A WELL-WATERED

Garden

A Book of Poems

Patricia Antoinette Diaz

www.xulonpress.com

AUTHOR BIO

Patricia A. Diaz

*P*atty has been married to Frank Diaz Jr. for forty-three years. Together they have been blessed with one son, Anthony M. Diaz. They also are blessed to have many spiritual sons and daughters that the Lord has brought into their lives. They have attended Calvary Chapel South Bay for over thirty-three years and were fortunate to sit under the teaching of Pastor Steve and Gail Mays. Patty worked in the publishing industry for Pacific Bell Yellow Pages for over twenty years. She retired and became a full time Homemaker, Homeschooler, Women's Ministry volunteer, Children's Ministry volunteer, and Writer. Her desire is to bring glory to her Lord and Savior, Jesus Christ, in all aspects of her life.

ENDORSEMENTS

Patty is a woman who is a devoted wife and mother first and foremost. Her love for Jesus is shown in her everyday life of reaching out and simply being a friend and a mentor to whomever God brings into her life. I have been blessed and enriched by her friendship for over thirty years. She truly understands ministry and has been a co-labor with me in Women's Ministry at Calvary Chapel South Bay from its beginning. Her unique gift of taking the truths of God's word and putting them into poems has encouraged and uplifted me each time I have read them. May these poems help you in your journey of life and keep you looking up.

Gail Mays
Author and Conference Speaker

Patty and I have been friends for over twenty-seven years. She has been my spiritual mentor and an amazing example of a godly woman to me. We served in AWANA's Women's Ministry, Discipleship Training, and Bible Study for many years together. Her gift of writing poems blessed, inspired, and encouraged me as she shared them with me. God has blessed her with an ability to share God's love, empathy, comfort, and encouragement through her writings. I pray that you might be blessed as I have through them.
Karen Haleck
Woman's Ministry

I have known Patty for over twenty-five years now and have walked through many "seasons" of life together. She has been to me a co-laborer, a servant, a friend…but most of all a sister in Christ. Over the years she has exhorted me, prayed for me, encouraged me, and helped me to be a better Christian. Many times through her poems I have received a word of hope or help at just the perfect time. God has blessed her with many gifts and I am forever grateful she readily shares these with the body of Christ. Thank you dear friend!
Suzie Park
Woman's Ministry Leadership CCSB

"...Everyone who is called by My name, and whom I have created for My glory, whom I have formed, even whom I have made." Isaiah 43:7 NASB

God created mankind for His good purpose. I have had the privilege of watching Patty live out her Christian walk for over twenty-five years seeking, defining, and practicing that purpose in her life. Her love for His people and her desire to shepherd and encourage them has been shared through her poetic words for many years. I encourage her readers to grab a cup of tea, cozy up in their favorite spot, and enjoy the refreshing lyrics of her writings.

Linda Kalama
Women's Worship Leader CCSB

I have known and served in ministry with Patty for over twenty years now. She is known to many as a strong woman of faith. She uses her gift of poetry to touch your heart. Her words will lift your spirits, inspire your walk with God, and bring you hope for another day.

Laura De Jong
Women's Ministry CCSB

Serving in the healthcare industry, I can appreciate the importance of addressing the physical and emotional matters of the heart. Patty skillfully uses her gift with words to compose poems that minister grace, hope, and God's love to the reader. Some of her poems were written during a time of personal pain and loss rendering writings that poignantly deal with pain and conclude with joy as the one is reminded of triumphant hope found in God's sovereign love. The Lord's grace and kindness flows into Patty's daily walk as she encourages young couples in the marriage ministry, mentors young mothers, and participates in the leadership of the Women's Ministry. She faithfully cared for her sick brother and led him to the Lord before he moved to heaven. I have known Patty for twenty years as we both attend Calvary Chapel South Bay. Perhaps the strongest commendation for Patty, the author and my close friend, is that she lives out the principles that produce her works. Her poems are not mere rhythmic words; they are compositions birthed from a deep love for her Lord and Savior Jesus Christ.

Laura Richardson
RN,
BSN, PHN

What an amazing woman and talented writer! I have been blessed by gifts of poetry over the last several years from Patty. One particular poem sits on my counter. On the days when I've done my best but my best doesn't feel enough, the days I don't feel loved or lovely I read, "One of a Kind." Patty reminds me of the words of Psalm 139:14, "I am fearfully and wonderfully made." I am God's design. I am His plan and He designs perfectly.

Dr. Deborah Beach,
Patty's Chiropractor

For those needing words of comfort and encouragement during difficult times, my sister's insightful poetry will be the perfect medicine.

Mary M. Link
Real Estate Broker
Island Link Realty

When I said a prayer from the depths of my heart…God answered in the most beautiful way when He sent me Patty. My life has been wonderfully blessed by the love, care, and godly example she has shown me. She has encouraged me in all areas of life and living with her love and knowledge of Scripture. It is my prayer that these poems give you even just a glimpse of the amazing woman of God she is.

Elaine Penrod Wenda
Patty's daughter in the faith

I have known Patty for over twenty years. She has been a dear special friend, a mother in the faith to me, and a god-mother to my daughter Phoebe. I have been blessed to serve and co-labor with her in Women's Ministry at Calvary Chapel South Bay for many years. She is a spiritual mom and sister to so many and her gift of writing poetry brings you close to God's heart. For years I have read and collected many of her poems. This book of poetry is extra special because it was inspired by God through the Holy Spirit. It is uplifting, encouraging, and gives you hope. With much love and blessings,

Arlene Coronel
Senior Manager of Human Resources CSU Chancellors Office
Women's Ministry Leadership CCSB

SUMMARY OF A WELL-WATERED GARDEN

"The LORD will guide you always, He will satisfy your needs in a sun-scorched land and strengthen your frame. You will be like a well-watered garden, and like a spring whose waters never fail." Isaiah 58:11 NIV

A Well-Watered Garden is a combination of scripture and inspirational poetry. This book was written to celebrate our victory in and through the Lord Jesus Christ, encourage those who are weary in their walk upon Calvary Road, lift up those who are discouraged in their trials, tribulations, and sufferings, and to bring glory to the LORD God Almighty, our Abba Father, who is our faithful Father in every situation, circumstance, and season of our life. If you are drawing from

His wells of salvation by placing your faith and trust in the Lord and Savior of our souls, Jesus Christ, then you will be that well-watered garden whose waters never fail.

TABLE OF CONTENTS

"The LORD will guide you always; He will satisfy your needs in a sun-scorched land and strengthen your frame. You will be like a well-watered garden, and like a spring whose waters never fail." Isaiah 58:11 NIV

A Well-Watered Garden

O Lord, make my soul satisfied even in a sun-scorched land,
Make me a well-watered garden in the palm of Your hand.

A spring whose waters never fail but flourish,
I am fed by Your wells of salvation that always nourish.

And Lord, may I rejoice and sorrow no more,
Knowing You are my Savior, the One that I adore.

Even though these struggles have made me weak,
Torrents of Your living water I shall continually seek.

Lord, strengthen my bones and establish my frame,
I know I am more than a conqueror in Jesus' name.

I am like a well-watered garden whose waters
never fail indeed,
For it is upon Your faithfulness, Lord, I shall
always feed.

"Who can find a virtuous wife? For her worth is far above rubies." Proverbs 31:10

A Woman of Virtue

A woman of virtue can easily be found,
Find a woman in God's Word and her life will be sound.

Rubies cannot compare to her value and her worth,
She is the most precious thing upon this entire earth.

The heart of her husband safely trusts in his wife,
She does him good not evil all the days of her life.

She willingly works all the while with her hands,
And on the promises of God is where she faithfully stands.

She uses godly wisdom to guide her in all things,
She never neglects to honor her Savior the King of Kings.

To those in need she gladly gives,
Her goal is to serve others for as long as she lives.

She is clothed in strength, honor, and love,
She is wise as a serpent, yet gentle as a dove.

The bread of idleness is not upon her tongue,
She watches over her household until every-
thing is done.

Her children rise up and call her blessed,
Her husband praises her for she gives him
her best.

Many daughters have done well, but she excels
them all,
For she hears the Lord's voice and follows
His call.

Charm is deceitful and vain beauty is passing,
But a woman who fears the Lord has a beauty
that is lasting.

For honoring her Lord she shall be praised,
She sits at His feet with her hands to Him raised.

A woman of virtue is a prize to behold,
More priceless than choice silver and more
sought after than pure gold.

"My brethren, count it all joy when you fall into various trials, knowing that the testing of your faith produce patience." James 1:2

All the While

My brethren, count it all joy as you go through every trial,
For the testing of your faith produces patience all the while.

Your faith is the substance that is more precious than gold,
It is that which the Lord has given you to stand and be bold.

And when gold passes through fire it becomes gold that is pure,
By submitting to God in the trial, you glorify Him as you endure.

God has ordered all things according to the counsel of His own will,
He shall meet every one of your needs and your cup He shall fill.

As the fire grows hotter, thank the Lord for the test,
Then praise Him as you enter into His arms of rest.

Your patient faith will be perfected not lacking
anything,
Enabling you to trust the Lord as your sover-
eign King.

Yes, my brethren, count it all joy as you go
through every trial,
For Jesus is your companion who carries you
through it all the while.

"Now may the God of hope fill you with all joy and peace in believing, that you may abound in hope by the power of the Holy Spirit." Romans 15:13

Always and Forever I Abound in Hope

Always and forever, I abound in hope in You, Lord, Your way,
I fall into Your arms of grace and mercy provided for me every day.

No matter what my eyes see my heart has greater sight,
Therefore, I walk by faith in You and trust You day and night.

Your way only leads to abundant joy and perfect peace,
You have overcome the world Jesus and You cause the storms to cease.

As I go through this life believing You will work it all out for my good,
Because my hope is ever abounding in You Lord, as I know it should.

It is by the power of Your Holy Spirit that this
I am able to do,
Always and forever precious Lord, I abound
in hope in You.

"The eternal God is your refuge, and underneath are the everlasting arms..." Deuteronomy 33:27

Another Sleepless Night

O Lord, I cannot face another sleepless night,
Therefore, to Your everlasting arms I will take my flight.

Only because You are with me can I face those lonely hours ahead,
Considering not the sleep that is lost I will place my mind on You instead.

At times it seems as if I am in an endless dark valley that is deep,
And that is when my heart is crushed and I begin to weep.

Through the crushing of my life I know my flesh is passing away,
That Jesus would be what remains in it each and every day.

I can choose to be depressed or turn this care into a prayer,
I can walk in His strength or crawl in utter despair.

The only way I can face another sleep-
less night,
Is to know Your everlasting arms are holding
me tight.

"For I know the thoughts that I think toward you, says the LORD, thoughts of peace and not of evil, to give you a future and a hope." Jeremiah 29:11

As I Sit

As I sit and watch my dreams begin to die,
My heartbreaks, I hang my head, and I cry.

Once again I fall before Your throne of mercy completely broken,
And then I humbly listen for Your still small voice that is spoken.

I sit and wait upon You, Lord; I must be very still,
Allowing my faith to grow and my spirit to know Your will.

I am thankful for everything that Your sovereignty may bring,
I continue to proclaim to the world that You are my ruling King.

You are my Savior and my God who has numbered all of my days.
The Lord of all of my life and who knows all of my ways,

As I sit and watch my dreams die,
I have no need to ask You, Lord, why?

The plans and thoughts You have for me are
greater than I could ever dream,
Thoughts of peace and not of evil no matter
how the circumstances seem.

"I love the LORD because He hears my prayers and answers them. Because He bends down and listens, I will pray as long as I breathe."
Psalm 116:1-2 TLB

As Long as I Breathe

As long as I breathe I will call out my prayer,
Because You bend down and listen with loving care.

You are faithful and true to answer every request,
With just the right response: a no, wait, or a yes.

A no means You have something better for me,
A wait means I am to trust as by faith not sight I see.

Then finally a yes means Your will be done this day,
Oh how I love You, Lord, for me there is no other way.

"Looking for the blessed hope and glorious appearing of our great God and Savior Jesus Christ." Titus 2:13

Before I Met Jesus

Before I met Jesus my heart was black with sin,
But now that He is my Savior, a new heart beats within.

Before I met Jesus I had no inner peace,
But now that He is my Savior, the turmoil must cease.

Before I met Jesus my life had no rest,
But now that He is my Savior, I have heaven's best.

Before I met Jesus I couldn't even cope,
But now that He is my savior, I have eternal hope.

Before I met Jesus my life was doomed to the end,
But now that He is my Savior, He is my closest friend.

Before I met Jesus my whole life had fallen apart,
But now that He is my Savior, He has healed every part.

"Behold, the eye of the LORD is on those who fear Him, on those who hope in His mercy, to deliver their soul from death, and to keep them alive in famine. Our soul waits for the LORD; He is our help and our shield. For our heart shall rejoice in Him, because we have trusted in His holy name." Psalm 33:18-21

Behold, the Eye of the LORD

Behold, the eye of the LORD is on those who fear Him,
On those who hope in His mercy as they flee from sin.

To deliver their soul from death and keep them alive,
They wait on Him even in famine; He is how they survive.

They have placed their trust in His holy name,
His mercy is upon them for He took their blame.

He is their help and their mighty shield,
Onto Him their life they do yield.

Their hearts rejoice in Him all the day long,
He is their strength and their constant song.

Beloved, the Lord is watching over you,
Place Him first in your life whatever you do.

"The LORD is near unto them that are of a broken heart and saves such as have a contrite spirit." Psalm 34:18

Broken Hearted

Broken hearted, with so many dreams that have died,
I am broken hearted, this cannot be denied.

Father, You said that You are near to them of a broken heart,
That You would never leave them nor from them would You ever depart.

You allowed Your heart to be broken and completely shattered on that day,
As You laid the sins of the world upon Your Son, for there was no other way.

You gave Jesus as Lord and Savior to heal all hearts that are broken,
And a relationship with You by the life giving words that You have spoken.

You proclaimed Your love to all broken hearts when You gave Your Son,
He is that free gift that restores and revives the hearts of everyone.

For I know I can place my broken heart safely
in Your hand,
You will heal it when before You I
humbly stand.

"Then Jesus said to His disciples, 'If anyone desires to come after Me, let him deny himself, and take up his cross, and follow Me.'" Matthew 16:24

Calvary Road

It takes a servant's heart of love to walk the Calvary Road,
To lay your burdens down there and ask Jesus to take the load.

It takes a life resigned to die to self each new day,
To pick up your cross and follow Jesus according to God's way.

It takes two willing hands raised in total surrender,
To minister to others all that is merciful, gracious, and tender.

It takes someone submitted humbly to God in order to lead,
To teach the Word of God by dispersing His Gospel Seed.

It takes a committed mind, soul, and a will
to obey,
To answer the call that God has placed upon
your life today.

It takes just what you have been given for
God's precious flock,
To lead His sheep in holy worship, which glo-
rifies salvation's Rock.

Jesus always gives you what it takes to walk
the Calvary Road,
He will replace your burdens with His bless-
ings by the truckload.

"She opens her mouth with wisdom and on her tongue is the law of kindness."
Proverbs 31:26

Days Gone By

As I sit and ponder days gone by,
I am reminded that my God knows all the reasons why.

Why the afflictions, why the sorrow,
Why not today, why I am to hope in tomorrow.

Why sometimes loss, why sometimes gain,
Why sometimes joy, why sometimes pain.

But I believe all things work together for my good,
Regardless of how often I have been tried and misunderstood.

Therefore, words that are wise I shall choose to speak,
Followed by actions of kindness and deeds that are meek.

For I know my God is perfecting in me a greater faith in Him,
He is carving a larger place inside of me that He may dwell in.

And this is more than enough to keep me content,
Knowing my days serving my Lord are well spent.

As I sit and ponder by gone days,
I am thankful for all of my God's merciful ways.

"But God demonstrates His own love toward us, in that while we were still sinners, Christ died for us. Romans 5:8

Dear Lord

Dear Lord, You are the One who puts a smile on my face,
Because You laid Your life down for me and took my place.

You are with me no matter what state that I am in,
Your unconditional love for me has blotted out my sin.

You are the One who never takes His eyes off of me,
Your thoughts for me are more than the sands of the sea.

You are the One who answers all of my prayers,
You always lift my burdens, provide my needs, and attend to all my cares.

Dear Lord, You are the One who puts a smile on my face,
You show me Your great mercy and Your unending grace.

"Casting all your care upon Him, for He cares for you." 1 Peter 5:7

Dear to my Heart

Lord, this is something so dear to my heart,
It is a deep concern that is tearing me apart.

I know the solution is just a prayer away,
Keep me faithful as I wait for that day.

Your strength is all I have to go on,
I know You will rescue me before too long.

I am in the place where You want me to be,
Positioned right where I will see Your total victory.

Lord, this is something so dear to my heart,
I give You this concern and allow You to do Your part.

"My flesh and my heart fail; but God is the strength of my heart and my portion forever."
Psalm 73:26

Deeper

Take me deeper, Lord, in my relationship with You,
Take me deeper as it is only Your love I seek and pursue.

Draw me closer, Lord, to You every night and every day,
Draw me closer as I put my trust in You all the way.

Lord, You know my flesh and my heart they fail,
But You are the strength in my life that shall prevail.

You, Lord, are my portion, all that I will ever need,
Fulfilling Your Word according to Your sovereign speed.

All of Your promises are, "Yes" and "Amen,"
You, Jesus, are eternally my "Faithful Forever Friend."

Draw me closer that I am transformed is what I pray,
Draw me closer, Lord, that Your will I would obey.

Take me deeper in fellowship and communion with You,
Take me deeper in the knowledge of all that You can do.

"Delight yourself also in the LORD, and He shall give you the desires of your heart."
Psalm 37:4

Delight Yourself in the LORD

Delight yourself in the LORD and take pleasure in all that He has done,
He is constantly working in your life through the sacrifice of His Son.

Know that every good and perfect gift is from heaven above,
And that what He has allowed in your life is because of his great love.

Rejoice in all things for He is working them out for your good,
Conforming you into the image of Jesus; let this be fully understood.

His promise for you, as you delight in Him, is to give you your desire,
To satisfy you beyond your hopes and to ignite in you the Holy Spirit's fire.

Delight yourself in the LORD and your heart's desire will be granted,

Then upon His plans for you, always let your feet be firmly planted.

"Whenever I am afraid, I will trust in You. In God I have put my trust. I will not fear. What can flesh do to me?" Psalm 56:3&4

Do Not Be Afraid

Do not be afraid, I Am your shield, your exceedingly great reward,
I Am your God almighty, your loving Savior, and your sovereign Lord.

Do not tremble as on My promises you stand,
I will be your mighty warrior and hide you in My sovereign hand.

Fear not, for My thoughts for you are good and wondrous is My plan,
I Am your constant Redeemer, the Lord Righteous I Am.

Do not stagger nor worry as My Word you are standing upon,
I Am the only One who will never forsake you whom you may lean on.

Do not be afraid, I Am your shield, your exceedingly great reward,
Beloved, knit your heart to Mine and with Me be in one accord.

"Be angry, and do not sin. Mediate within your heart on your bed, and be still." Psalm 4:4

Do Not Sin

Be angry and do not sin,
Let the peaceable fruit of righteousness reign you in.

Meditate within your heart on your bed and be still,
Put your trust in the Lord and you will know His will.

I will both lie down in peace and sleep,
For my soul, O Lord, You forever keep.

I shall offer the sacrifice of praise to You,
You will remove my anger no matter what they do.

Know that the Lord will fight the battle that you're in,
You can be angry but you shall not sin.

Give that emotion to the Lord who, no matter what, loves you,
For anger will only rot your bones all the way through.

Be angry and sin not
The Lord has cast my lot.

"The eternal God is your refuge, and underneath are the everlasting arms…"
Deuteronomy 33:27

Everlasting Arms

Everlasting arms, from the beginning without end,
My God, my Savior, my Commander, my forever friend.

He is eternally concerned with everything that happens to me,
He has orchestrated my life that I might have spiritual eyes to see.

That I might behold the vision of His glory and His supernatural power,
That strengthens my life to live for Him, day by day and hour by hour.

Giving me an insight to His sovereignty, which lovingly watches over me,
And allows me a personal relationship with Him, the eternal God Almighty.

The eternal God is my refuge, my shelter, and my hiding place,
He is my high tower, my cleft in the rock and my saving grace.

I know my trials are hand picked lovingly by
Him exclusively for me,
And that they are entrusted to me for my
growth by His sovereignty.

Everlasting, never ending, full of compassion,
arms of love,
My eternal God who is my refuge and who is
over heaven above.

"Who being the brightness of His glory and the express image of His person, and upholding all things by the word of His power, when He had by Himself purged our sins, sat down at the right hand of the Majesty on high."
Hebrews 1:3

Express Image

Jesus is the express image of His Father above,
He is the gift of His Father's unending love.

He is the giver of all life and servant of all,
His joy was to die for us and redeem us from the fall.

Jesus teaches us to be a slave,
From the example of all He gave.

The good of others is His desire,
His life is ablaze with sacrificial fire.

He did not come to be served but rather to serve,
And to free each of us from the prisons that we deserve.

First you must lose your life if your life you
want to gain,
For living only for yourself will only cause
turmoil and pain.

He purged our sins and now sits at the Father's
right hand,
And His thoughts for us are more than every
grain of sand.

The express image of His Father above,
Jesus, the greatest giver of life and of love.

"…if you have faith as a mustard seed, you will say to this mountain, 'Move from here to there,' and it will move, and nothing will be impossible for you." Matthew 17:20

Faith as a Mustard Seed

Faith as a mustard seed,
That is the kind of faith you need.

For if mustard seed faith is properly tended it will flourish and grow,
Nothing can shake it regardless of how hard the wind might blow.

God will allow each gale to come that your faith becomes stronger,
So that doubt and fear would be kept from plaguing you any longer.

Thus, mustard seed faith will produce the largest tree of them all,
Genuinely strong for its roots are in Jesus, therefore, it cannot fall.

Mustard seed faith can say to the mountain, "Get out of my way,"
And according to God's will it shall stand victoriously every day.

Spreading its branches out so others may find
their rest,
And feeding the weary luscious fruit that is
only God's best.

Faith as a mustard seed might start out
very small,
Trust in God and He will cause it to be the
greatest of all.

"For I, the LORD your God, will hold your right hand, saying unto you, 'Fear not, I will help you.'" Isaiah 41:13

Fear Not

Fear not, for I the LORD am your God who will hold your right hand,
You are kept by My power, and by My command.

Fear not, for I the LORD am always for you and I will never leave you,
I will sustain you in your darkest hour and I will see you through.

Fear not, for I the LORD am God Almighty who is on your side,
You can take your refuge under My wings and there you can hide.

Fear not, for I the LORD am He who will give you total victory,
Put all your faith, all your trust, and all your hopes in Me.

Fear not, My beloved precious child; just place your hand in Mine,
For I the LORD will help you with My awesome power that is divine.

"Trust in the LORD and do good; dwell in the land, and feed on His faithfulness."
Psalm 37:3

Feed on His Faithfulness

Trust in the LORD and do the good things He has created especially for you,
Occupy the land and be about your Father's business in everything you do.

Feed upon His faithfulness as in Him you take delight and great pleasure,
He promises to give you the deep desires of your heart, His priceless treasure.

Commit all your ways to the LORD as you trust in His sovereignty,
He is your Faithful Father, Merciful Savior, and LORD God Almighty.

Deny yourself, pick up your cross, and follow Him in every circumstance,
For in this life nothing happens to you by accident or by mere chance.

It is all to serve His divine purpose as you sojourn on planet earth,
Through Jesus' sacrifice on the cross He has given you your worth.

Trust in the LORD, His beloved, and do His
will His way,
Feed upon His faithfulness, His unconditional
love for you every day.

"But thanks be to God, who gives us victory through our Lord Jesus Christ."
1 Corinthians 15:57

Fire and Rain

I've been through fire and I survived the rain,
I've been through sorrow and I endured the pain.

That which God has allowed in my life has forever left its mark,
It has brought me into His light and taken me forever from the dark.

Reflecting His love for me and shinning it upon my face,
Transforming me by the power of His amazing grace.

I've been through fire, accompanied by torrential rain.
I've been through sorrow, resulting in tremendous pain.

However, this one thing remains to be that which is forever true,
God is faithful to make me victorious as He guides me through.

"Yet for love's sake I rather appeal to you…"
Philemon 9

For Love's Sake

Yet for love's sake I appeal to you according
to God's grace,
Your steps have been ordered by Him and
He's put you in your place.

Walk therefore in His compassion what-
ever you do,
For His mercy that is beyond measure has
been lavished upon you.

Know this, that every good thing that is within
you is because of Him,
Let this profound yet simple fact penetrate
Your soul deep within.

Receive anyone, who is in Christ as your
beloved friend,
Placing between you the sacrifice of Jesus as
your beginning and end.

I appeal to you dear one for love's sake,

Let Jesus Christ be the Holy Communion you
together partake.

"Surely He has borne our griefs and carried our sorrows…" Isaiah 53:4

For This I Have Jesus

"For this I have Jesus," is what the Lord said to me,
I didn't understand it because at first I couldn't see.

For a time of sorrow accompanied by painful grief had come my way,
It felt as if I couldn't go on; I prayed, "Lord, please revive me today."

My pain was so severe and so deep within my heart,
It was as if something had reached in and removed the most precious part.

I found myself crippled and grasping for air,
I couldn't go on for I was filled with too much despair.

But I was reminded by Your Spirit that You too have been in this same place,
And that Your tears of agony were shed for me because of Your loving grace.

For You are familiar and intimately acquainted
with my sorrow and my pain,
You promised that if I cast it upon You, Lord,
Your peace I would gain.

You said each day I trusted You, Jesus, You
would ease my pain and grief,
And that in Your everlasting arms of love, my
Lord, I would find my relief.

Then You promised to heal my heart so I
could go on,
Reminding me, "For this I have Jesus," as my
constant song.

Yes, "For this I have Jesus" who sacrificed His
life for mine,
And who faithfully bares my pain and sorrow
beyond the end of time.

"Against You, You only, have I sinned and done this evil in Your sight…" Psalm 51:4

Forgive Me Lord

Forgive me Lord, for I have sinned against You alone,
Cleanse me Lord that I may come before Your holy throne.

My confession is ever before You,
Lord, it is Your mercy that I daily pursue.

Blot out all my sins and please hold back all that I deserve,
Declare me righteous by the blood of Jesus that You I might serve.

Purge me with hyssop and I shall be clean,
It is through Jesus that Your grace I have seen.

Wash me in Jesus' sacrificial blood and I shall be white as snow,
Let Your forgiveness be the one and only thing that I know.

Create in me, O God, a clean heart,
Renew a right spirit in me and give me a fresh start.

Lord, teach me Your holy Way,
I will turn from wickedness every day.

Forgive me Lord, for I have sinned against
You alone,
Open my lips to worship You before Your
holy throne.

"...please let us fall into the hand of the
LORD, for His mercies are great..."
2 Samuel 24:14

From My Father's Hand

I know everything that is happening to me,
Is from my Father's hand that I might be
set free.

What had bound me up this day,
The fiery trial has burned away.

When I thought I was abandoned where
I stand,
I looked up and there I saw my Father's hand.

For His hand isn't trying to inflict any pain,
His hand upholds me and removes my shame.

It is His hand of love that gently corrects me,
That I can be all that He has planned for
me to be.

My Father's hand I have no need to ever fear,
His hand never turns me away, it draws
me near.

Yes, my Father's hand will change and transform me,
Into the image of Jesus who is my total victory.

"For God is not unjust to forget your work and labor of love which you have shown toward His name, in that you have ministered to the saints, and do minister." Hebrews 6:10

God is Not Unjust

For God is not unjust to forget your work and labor of love,
He will continue to pour out upon you His blessings from above.

His storehouse is filled with everything you need,
And He will repay you abundantly for every good deed.

For you have done this in His name as you ministered to every saint,
Not growing weary in doing good nor allowing your heart to faint.

You did it not by your power but through the power of the Lord,
Therefore it is from Him that you shall receive your reward.

For God is not unjust to ever forget about you,
He will always bless your labor of love, the work that you do.

"Be strong and of good courage, do not fear nor be afraid of them; for the Lord your God, He is the One who goes with you. He will not leave you nor forsake you."
Deuteronomy 31:6

God Almighty

Be strong and of good courage, do not fear nor be afraid in any way,
For the Lord your God Almighty goes with you each and every day.

With them is the arm of flesh but with us is God Almighty, the holy One,
Who holds the universe together and freely gave us Jesus His dear Son.

Be strong and courageous; do not be dismayed,
God Almighty is right on time, He won't ever be delayed.

Fear not, beloved, whatever you do,
God Almighty will forever take care of you.

Never place any confidence in the power of man,
God Almighty will always make a way; you know He can.

God Almighty is with us even to the very end,
For He is the Lord God Almighty our Savior
and friend.

"And the Word became flesh and dwelt among us, and we beheld His glory, the glory as of the only begotten of the Father, full of grace and truth." John 1:14

God Became a Man

Jesus, God in the flesh, became a man to save you and me,
He joyfully left His throne in heaven to set us free.

It was His plan before the beginning of time,
He made eternal life with Him yours and mine.

The sacrifice that He freely gave we can receive,
Therefore, in His Son, Jesus Christ, we must believe.

We were born separated from God with the nature to sin,
Ask Jesus in your heart and His Spirit will abide within.

We can stand before our God completely justified,
Before His throne of grace, His mercy cannot be denied.

It is that simple and yet it is that profound,
It is the song of the universe the sweetest sound.

Let heaven and earth rejoice because God
became a man,
He demonstrated His amazing grace for us
fulfilling His plan.

"God in the midst of her, she shall not be moved; God shall help her, just at the break of dawn." Psalm 46:5

God in the Midst of Her

God is in the midst of her and she shall not be moved,
Because at Calvary, His love for her has been proved.

God through His awesome power shall help her just at the break of dawn,
The Son of Righteousness shall shine upon her and she shall journey on.

Though fiery darts of the enemy are flung at her she knows faith shall avail,
She stands in the victory that's been won for her and knows it shall never fail.

She is providentially positioned by God's amazing grace,
She knows the battle is His therefore the warfare she can face.

Even when the storms mount up and the winds blow a mighty gale,
She shall not be moved for God is in the midst of her she shall prevail.

God shall help her just at the break of dawn at
the end of night,
For it is His plan to grow her through it because
she is His delight.

"But no one says, 'Where is God my Maker
who gives songs in the night.'"
Job 35:10

God is My Maker

God is my Maker, who gives me a song in the
darkest night,
He gives me eagle's wings that I might take
my flight.

As I am singing and soaring in the heaven's above,
I am declaring my song of His incredible love.

God is my Maker, who knows everything
about me,
He breaks the chains that bind me and sets
me free.

God has given me His victory song therefore
I must sing,
He is my Maker, my Savior, my Lord, and
my King.

"For in the time of trouble He shall hide me in His pavilion; in the secret place of His tabernacle He shall hide me; He shall set me high upon a rock." Psalm 27:5

God Is

God is my fortress, my protector, and the wind beneath my wing,
God is my strength, my salvation, and He is my everything.

God is my provider, my secret place, and my endless power,
God is my pavilion, my rock, and my strong high tower,

God is my righteousness, my holiness, and my covering,
God is my ruler, my potentate, and my King.

God is my beginning, my end, my all, and my say,
God is my always, my forever, and God is my way.

"O Lord You have searched me and know me.
Psalm 139:1

God Knows Your Name

God knows your name,
He knit together your fragile frame.

He knows the number of hairs on your head,
He is aware of every word you have ever said.

He is intimately acquainted with you,
He knows just what you are going to do.

Your life is in His loving hands,
Live it as His Word commands.

God knows your name,
And it is for you that Jesus came.

"…Yes, I have loved you with an everlasting love…" Jeremiah 31:3

God's Love for You

God's love for you has always been,
It has no limits nor does it have any end.

His precious thoughts for you are to be treasured,
The good He has stored up for you cannot be measured.

The peace that He gives goes beyond human conception,
Guarding your heart and mind from all deception.

Fix your eyes upon His promises and upon them depend,
He is God almighty, thus you He shall always defend.

God's love for you is as the universe is vast,
It will never run out and will forever last.

"Love never fails…" 1 Corinthians 13:8

God's Love Will Never Stop

In the valley of love there is no bottom and on
the mountain of love there is no top,
God's agape love has no end; His love knows
no limit, and it will never stop.

God has shed His love abroad mightily abun-
dantly within my heart,
I am to dispense it liberally to all because it is
His love that has set me apart.

His love will last forever healing every wound,
every sorrow, every question, every time,
It is everlasting, enduring, steadfast, long suf-
fering, and totally divine.

His love never quits, doesn't get discouraged,
and doesn't let anything drop,
God's love will never hurt you, never leave
you, never fail you, and it will never stop.

"...Grace, mercy, and peace from God our Father and Jesus Christ our Lord."
1 Timothy 1:2

Grace, Mercy, and Peace

Grace, mercy, and peace clothed in Your glory, Lord, what a sight to see,
A complete pardon that justifies me and completely sets me free.

Withholding any punishment because You, Jesus, took my place,
That is the awesome vision set before me; Your mercy and Your grace.

I am amazed and speechless not knowing what to say,
For mere words cannot express my gratitude nor my love can they convey.

Therefore I gladly offer You my life and my free will,
Knowing You have everything under Your control, keeps my heart still.

My confidence is in You, Lord, who made the heavens and the earth,
Who called me into being and gave me my priceless worth.

Grace, mercy, and peace clothed in Your glory
freely given to me,
Transforms me and enables me to be all You
desire me to be.

"You brought us into the net; You laid affliction on our backs…but You brought us out to rich fulfillment." Psalm 66:11-12

Hands That Are Empty

Hands that are empty and a broken heart,
This affliction has completely torn me apart.

Yet, I know this affliction is for the benefit of me,
That I might have spiritual eyes that are ready to see.

The salvation of the Lord moving every day,
That is manifesting in me His most holy way.

The Lord is faithful to remove me out of this net,
For the boundaries of this trial have already been set.

I know nothing touches me that is outside of God's plan,
He will bring about a rich fulfillment as only He can.

Hands that are empty and a broken heart,
My God by His power will restore every part.

"Happy is the man who finds wisdom, and the man who gains understanding."
Proverbs 3:13

Happy is the Man

Happy is the man who finds wisdom from above,
Who gains understanding and God's agape love.

For the gain is better than fine silver and pure gold,
Wisdom is more precious than rubies; her value is untold.

All the things you may desire cannot compare with her,
Length of days is in her right hand so fair and so pure.

In her left hand she holds honor and riches,
Her ways are of pleasant dreams and prayerful wishes.

And all her paths are filled with peace,
She is a tree of life that will set you at ease.

Happy is the man who finds wisdom,
Who gains understanding of God's kingdom.

"He who overcomes shall inherit all things and I will be his God, and he shall be My son. Revelation 21:7

He Who Overcomes

He who overcomes shall inherit all things,
I will be his God, his King of Kings.

And he shall be My son,
By the sacrifice of the Holy One.

By the blood of the Lamb he has overcome,
By the work on the cross that Jesus has done.

He who overcomes shall inherit all things,
He will take his rest under My wings.

"May the LORD continually bless you with heaven's blessings as well as with human joy." Psalm 128:5 TLB

Heaven's Blessings

Heaven's blessings are an abundant gift You, Lord, faithfully give,
It is the Bread of Life that satisfies my soul and allows me to live.

And the joy that overflows my grateful heart revives me every day,
While it sustains me as I journey her on earth until You take me away.

For my greatest desire is to be before You face to face,
Where I will worship and adore You in that most holy place.

May the Lord continually bless you with heaven's blessings from above,
And may you know the immeasurable amount of His unconditional love.

"Let us be glad and rejoice and give Him glory, for the marriage of the Lamb has come and His wife has made herself ready. And to her it was granted to be arrayed in fine linen, clean and bright, for the fine linen is the righteous acts of the saints." Revelation 19:7&8

His Beautiful Bride

How precious is His Beautiful Bride,
Forever she shall remain by her Lord's side.

The marriage of the Lamb has come and His wife is ready,
The promise of His coming has made her confident and steady

Jesus' righteousness has cleansed her from all sin,
Thus, fine linen clean and bright she is forever clothed in.

Let us be glad and rejoice for His wife is the most beautiful thing,
She bows daily before her Lord acknowledging Him as her King.

Her relationship with Him has made her pure
and sweet,
And she has chosen to constantly sit at her
Lord's feet.

She has been promised and sealed by the
Spirit as His wife.
She has dedicated herself to the Lord and
given Him her life,

Let the saints say, "How precious is His
Beautiful Bride,"
For they know her every need He shall always
provide.

"Therefore I will look to the LORD; I will wait for the God of my salvation; my God will hear me." Micah 7:7

Homesick for You, LORD

O LORD, I am homesick for You,
I feel my time here on earth is past due.

Yet I will patiently wait for You to take me home,
I will look to You, LORD, and purpose in my heart never to roam.

You will hear me at all times of the day and night,
As I cry out to You, You make all things right.

I will wait for You, the God of my salvation, today,
O LORD, I am homesick for You; are You on Your way?

"Remembering without ceasing your work of faith, labor of love, and patience of hope in our Lord Jesus Christ in the sight of our God and Father." 1 Thessalonians 1:3

Hope in Christ

Hope in Christ all you who walk by faith and not by sight,
He will manifest His Spirit in you by His supernatural might.

Hope in Christ all you who labor in love for the Lord,
He will faithfully be your eternal reward.

Hope in Christ all you who are weary and heavy-laden,
He will carry your load; you will not be forsaken.

Hope in Christ all you who manifold trials befall,
He will carry you and deliver you through them all.

Hope in Christ all you who call upon His name,
He will forgive all your sins and remove your shame.

Hope in Christ all you who mourn in
great sorrow,
He will take your pain and give you joy for
tomorrow.

Hope in Christ all you who are waiting for His
return one day,
He will be your Lord and by His side you shall
always stay.

"How precious also are Your thoughts to me,
O God! How great is the sum of them!"
Psalm 139:17

How Precious Are Your Thoughts for Me

How precious are Your thoughts for me, O
God; how wondrous are Your ways,
You skillfully knitted all my parts together
and You have numbered all my days.

If I were to count Your thoughts for me they
would be more than the sands of the sea,
I am overwhelmed contemplating the fact that
You never take Your mind off of me.

You understand my thoughts afar off; You
know my rising up and my sitting down,
I am precious in Your eyes and You have set
me as a jewel in Your crown.

Marvelous are Your works; I will praise You
for I am fearfully and wonderfully made,
Precious are Your thoughts for me, O God; I
know Your love for me will never fade.

"Keep my soul, and deliver me; let me not be ashamed, for I put my trust in You."
Psalm 25:20

I am leaving it all up to You

Lord, I am leaving it all up to You,
There is absolutely nothing I can do.

Keep my soul and deliver me,
Keep me faithful and set me free.

My hands are completely tied,
Your providence cannot be denied.

You have allowed me to endure this painful test,
I am waiting on You because You know what is best.

I will put my trust in You, be quiet, and sit still,
Please, Lord, put me in the center of Your will.

I know this will hurt all the more,
As in Your time You open up this door.

Let me not be ashamed; let me not fall,
When I cry out to You, Lord, hear my call.

I am leaving it all up to You,
Do what it is You need to do.

"Then Jesus spoke to them again saying, 'I am the light of the world. He who follows Me shall not walk in darkness, but have the light of life.'" John 8:12

I Am the Light of the World

I am the Light of the world, there is no other way but by Me,
Don't walk in the darkness for I came to set you free.

Follow Me and you will have the light of life lighting your way,
I am the Alpha and Omega, therefore, by your side I will forever stay.

I came that you might have abundant life full of My glory,
I am the bright morning star and I am the greatest love story.

I love you with a love that knows no measure,
I went from the stable to the cross seeking you, My treasure.

I am the gift that first Christmas, which was freely given,
Receive Me as your Savior and from your sins be forgiven.

I will be your Lord and My grace will
follow you,
Accompanied by My mercy all your days
through.

I am the light of the world, beloved, follow Me,
Walk in the light of life and all darkness
must flee.

"…I am God Almighty; walk before Me and be blameless." Genesis 17:1

I Am the Lord God Almighty

I will lift your afflictions,
And break any addictions,
For I Am the Lord God Almighty.

I will remove your sadness,
And replace it with gladness,
For I Am the Lord God Almighty.

I will take your shattered heart,
And restore every part,
For I Am the Lord God Almighty.

I will banish every fear,
And wipe away every tear,
For I Am the Lord God Almighty.

I will protect and provide,
And always be by your side,
For I Am the Lord God Almighty.

I will speak and be heard,
And reveal My every Word,
For I Am the Lord God Almighty.

I will rebuke and chastise,
And by fire I will baptize,
For I Am the Lord God Almighty.

I will encourage and uplift,
And to your rescue I will be swift,
For I Am the Lord God Almighty.

I will hear you when you pray,
And answer you the best way,
For I Am the Lord God Almighty.

I will love you beyond belief,
And always be your relief,
For I Am your Lord God Almighty.

"I trust in Your unfailing love; my heart
rejoices in Your salvation. I will sing to the
LORD, for He has been good to me."
Psalm 13:5-6 NIV

I Trust in Your Unfailing Love

Oh LORD, I trust in Your unfailing love,
For it falls upon me as manna from above.

You are forever faithful, forever true,
I shall find my rest only in You.

In Your salvation my heart shall rejoice,
Daily I purpose to make Jesus my choice.

The way of the cross is the path for me,
In order to live in Your victory.

The LORD has been good to me, therefore to
Him I sing,
He is my sovereign ruler reigning forever as
my King.

Showering me with Your mercy from above,
I shall always trust in Your unfailing love.

"I wait for the LORD, my soul waits, and in His word do I hope. My soul waits for the LORD more than watchmen wait for the morning; indeed, more than the watchmen for the morning." Psalm 130:5-6

I Wait for the LORD

With anticipation I wait for the LORD when I pray,
I know He holds my future as I wake each day.

Having this confidence my soul waits for Him,
In His word there lies the hope that is within.

It is where this heart of mine finds rest and peace,
It is His word that causes the turmoil to cease.

My soul waits for the LORD,
He is my treasure, my great reward.

More than the watchmen wait for the morning to break,
My soul waits for Jesus every day as I awake.

"The LORD is on my side; I will not fear…"
Psalm 118:6

I Will Not Fear

The LORD is on my side; I will not fear,
When the storms come and the darkness is near.

You said You would never leave nor forsake,
I am depending upon You, my life is at stake.

I am trusting in You for You have always come
through,
In Your promises I am secure, for I know they
are true.

All understanding of man cannot fathom
Your peace,
As You calm the storms and cause the wind
to cease.

By the fountains of heaven overflowing
from above,
I am blessed and filled with Your abundant love.

No, I will not fear even in the midnight hour,
For You are on my side with Your awe-
some power.

"For if you remain completely silent at this time, relief and deliverance will arise for the Jews from another place, but you and your father's house will perish. Yet who knows whether you have come to the kingdom for such a time a this?" "...I will go...and if I perish, I perish!" Esther 4:14-16

If I Perish, Then I Perish

I shall do this thing for the Lord, for the Lord I cherish,
And if I should perish, then I perish.

For I know I have been called to the kingdom for such a time as this,
I shall go according to the Lord and according to the Lord I shall not miss.

God has allowed me to come to this ordained place,
And keep a divine appointment established by His grace.

I shall not fear what man can do to me,
I shall only fear the Living God who holds my eternity.

I shall do this for the Lord and if I perish,
I shall be ushered into heaven before the Lord
whom I cherish.

"In the beginning was the Word, and the Word was with God, and the Word was God." John 1:1

In the Beginning

In the beginning was the Word and the Word was with God, and the Word was God,
This is a true statement even though it may seem peculiar, even odd.

The precious Word of God became flesh and dwelt among us,
Thus we can celebrate every day the birth of our Lord Jesus.

His very humble beginnings lying in a lowly stable,
Yet, He is the King of Kings and Lord of Lords who is more than able.

God so loved the world that He gave His only begotten Son,
That He would be our Messiah, our Savior, and our Holy One.

In the beginning He stepped down from heaven's throne to come and rescue us,
Wonderful Counselor, Mighty God, Everlasting Father, Prince of Peace, He is Lord Jesus

"Yet, I will rejoice in the LORD, I will joy in the God of my salvation." Habakkuk 3:18

In the LORD I Shall Rejoice

I have made my choice,
In the LORD I shall rejoice.

Though the fig tree may not bloom,
I shall not be saddened by the sudden gloom.

Nor fruit be on the vines,
I shall meditate on good times.

Though the labor of the olive may fail,
I shall not be discouraged nor shall I wail.

And the fields yield no food,
I won't lose my joy nor shall I sit and brood.

Though the flock may be cut off from the fold,
I know my Savior's hand I shall always hold.

And there is no herd in the stall,
I shall not stumble nor shall I fall.

For the LORD God is my strength who gives
me hinds' feet,
He makes me to walk upon high places where
He and I always meet.

Though the fig tree may not bloom,
Nevertheless, because of Jesus I have escaped
from all doom.

I have made my choice,
In the LORD I shall rejoice.

"Both riches and honor come from You, and You reign over all. In Your hand is power and might; in Your hand it is to make great and to give strength to all." 1 Chronicles 29:12

In Your Hands

In Your hands is the safest place to be,
It is the place where we find rest and total victory.

In Your hands is our secure hiding place,
It is the place where we find Your amazing grace.

In Your hands is the place of our strength,
It is the place where Your love for us has no height, width, or length.

In Your hands is where we want to always be,
It is the place where, with unveiled eyes, we can see Your Majesty.

"Yet in all these things we are more than conquerors through Him who loved us." Romans 8:37

Invincible

You are invincible because of Jesus' shed blood,
In the day of trouble He will save you from the storm's flood.

Nothing that comes against you will ever succeed,
For the King of Kings will deliver you with God's speed.

All your days have been numbered and are in His hand,
Nothing can happen without His sovereign command.

Rest in this promise with His blessed assurance,
The Lord of Hosts will always be your life's insurance.

We are more than conquerors through Jesus our Lord,
He has defeated the enemy with His two-edged sword.

He has filled you with His Holy Spirit; His supernatural power,
Therefore fear not, beloved, He is your abiding strong tower.

Know that God is for you and has given you eternal life with Him
You are invincible by His sacrifice so let His Spirit rule you within.

"If you ask anything in My name, I will do it." John 14:14

Jesus Name

The enemy has been vanquished in Jesus' mighty name,
Therefore, his lies and attacks must cease and refrain.

Your life will never be the same,
When you speak Jesus' precious name.

It is because of you dear one that He came,
Find your peace in Jesus' wonderful name.

He knows all about you, every inch of your frame,
For all power dwells in Jesus' sovereign name.

The enemy can no longer put you to shame,
He must vanish at the mention of Jesus' holy name.

No longer do you need to bare any blame,
When you repent in Jesus' merciful name.

"You found his heart faithful before You..."
Nehemiah 9:8

Keep Me Faithful

Keep me faithful, Precious Lord, as I walk ahead,
You say, "Fear not I will help you, you have nothing to dread."

You have me in Your sovereign righteous right hand,
Sustaining me and causing me to triumphantly stand.

All Your promises are true and just what I need,
The answer to my every cry is in Your providential speed.

Keep me faithful, Precious Lord, is what I continue to pray,
As I hold on to You and Your word just one more day.

The enemy of my soul would have me think he has won,
But I know he's been defeated by Jesus, Your only begotten Son.

For I am a pilgrim on a journey to heaven my
real home,
With You by my side as my guide I shall never
be alone.

And that this matter that concerns me has been
settled by You in eternity,
Keep me faithful, Precious Lord, as I walk the
way of Calvary.

"For whom He foreknew, He also predestined to be conformed to the image of His Son…"
Romans 8:29

Life This Side of Heaven

When life this side of heaven isn't what we want it to be,
Remember, it is but for a moment and not for eternity.

It is only the place where we are planted and asked to grow,
Letting Jesus be the image we conform to and who we truly know.

It is where we are providentially tested, proven, and tried,
Where we come to the end of ourselves as self is totally denied.

Thus, life this side of heaven is to be lived by us in constant prayer,
In doing so, we unburden ourselves and give the Lord all our care.

It is a place where our faith is increased as we wait,
Allowing us to act on the promises of God and not to hesitate.

The place we learn to trust in Jesus and not to walk by sight,
Then to follow God's Word by His power and His might.

Life this side of heaven is but a moment to praise and glorify Him,
One day we shall enter heaven and eternity with Jesus shall begin.

"For our light affliction, which is but for a moment, is working for us a far more exceeding and eternal weight of glory."
2 Corinthians 4:17

Light Afflictions

Remember this truth, our light afflictions are but for a moment,
And that heaven is our home because of the Lord's atonement.

These trials are working for us a far more exceeding weight of glory,
That we might grow in the knowledge of the Lord's great love story.

The work that needs to be done goes deep within our very core,
When it is done it allows us to trust in the Lord all the more.

Beloved, God so loved you and me that He freely gave,
His precious gift, Jesus Christ, that our lives He might save.

There is no greater love known to any man,
Than to lay down your life and follow God's plan.

Our light afflictions will someday all pass away,
Then in eternity with Jesus we will forever stay.

"All we like sheep have gone astray; we have turned, every one, to his own way; and the LORD has laid on Him the iniquity of us all." Isaiah 53:6

Like Sheep Going Astray

For we were like helpless lost sheep going astray,
We were wandering without direction our own way.

God laid on Jesus all of our iniquity, our black sin,
That we could be saved and have fellowship with Him

Now we have returned to the Shepherd and Overseer of our soul.
Our life we have placed in Jesus' hands and it is under His control.

We are no longer to the enemy easy prey,
For we follow the Good Shepherd every day.

We trust Him as our Savior and our Caretaker,
Because we know He is our LORD and our Maker.

For we were like helpless lost sheep wandering and going astray,
But we have returned to Jesus our Good Shepherd, the only way.

"He who continually goes forth weeping bearing seed for sowing shall doubtless come again with rejoicing…"Psalm 126:6

Liquid Prayers

My tears have multiplied dear Lord; they are without number,
They fall on my pillow as I lay my head to slumber.

You promise all those who go forth weeping bearing precious seed,
Shall come again rejoicing because You will meet their every need.

My tears have fallen like a torrential rain,
They have flowed like a river to wash away my pain.

As I cry out to You, dear Lord, to answer every liquid prayer,
You show forth Your amazing grace and lift away my every care.

My tears are so precious to You, Lord, that You save every one,
They are liquid prayers that cry out for Your will to be done.

I thank You for all the tears that You have
allowed me to weep,
For I know every promise You have made is
a promise You will keep.

My liquid prayers are bearing seed for sowing
as my tears begin to fall,
I come again rejoicing because You, Lord,
have answered them all.

"But without faith it is impossible to please Him for he who comes to God must believe that He is, and that He is a rewarder of those who diligently seek Him." Hebrews 11:6

Lord I Believe

Lord, I believe in You and I believe that You are,
I believe that You made the earth and every heaven's star.

I believe that Your plans for me are for good filled with an expectant hope,
I believe that Your Spirit fills me and enables me to continually cope.

I believe Jesus died for me, that He rose from the dead on the third day,
I believe He intercedes on my behalf and my sins are washed away.

I believe You reward me as You I diligently seek,
I believe that my faith in You will be the loudest words I speak.

Lord, I believe that You are God the Almighty King,
I believe that You are creator and ruler over everything.

"But now, O LORD, You are our Father; we are the clay, and You our potter; and all we are the work of Your hand." Isaiah 64:8

LORD, You are the Potter

LORD, You are the potter and I am the clay,
Make me a vessel of honor able to serve You this day.

Mold me and make me as You turn the wheel,
Do what is necessary, no matter how I feel.

If there are imperfections and the clay has a mar,
In Your hands, LORD, do what is good and remove any scar.

Make me a vessel of honor fit to serve You,
And create a work in me that is brand new.

Allow me to sit in my Master's loving hand,
And use me to lead others to the promise land.

LORD, You are the potter and I am Your clay,
Make me a vessel for Your honor and use me today.

"Many are the afflictions of the righteous; but the LORD delivers him out of them all."
Psalm 34:19

Many Are the Afflictions of the Righteous

Upon the Lord's righteous many afflictions fall,
But the Lord God Almighty delivers him out of them all.

For afflictions are a teacher allowed in our life by our God above,
They instruct us in His sovereignty, His grace and His merciful love.

They chisel us into the image of Jesus, our dear Lord,
They are a benefit that unites us with our Father in one accord.

They are all within God's plan for our ultimate good,
You must never let this profound truth be misunderstood.

Beloved, fear not the many afflictions that so often come to call,
Remember that the Lord God Almighty will deliver you from them all.

"That the trial of your faith, being much more precious than of gold that perisheth though it be tried with fire, might be found unto praise and honor and glory at the appearing of Jesus Christ." 1 Peter 1:7 KJV

More Precious than Gold

As the rainbow comes after every storm, and after every shower,
God is on the throne and the universe is kept by His mighty power.

Know this, beloved one, as you enter into any trial,
God is still in control and He will sustain you all the while.

Yes, the rain shall fall on the good as on the evil,
And your life will face many storms, and much upheaval.

Remember His Word and all that you have been told,
That the trial of your faith is more precious than gold.

And that on the day you stand before your
Lord, your King,
You would present praise, honor, and glory as
your offering.

And having placed your trust and faith in Him
through every test,
Having stood and withstood the fiery trial you
enter into the Lord's rest.

And you shall rule and reign with Jesus as His
legal heir,
With no more sorrow, no more pain, and no
more despair.

"But thanks be to God, who gives us the victory through our Lord Jesus Christ."
1Corinthians 15:57

My Constant Victory

Lord, You will part the Red Sea for me,
You will always be my constant victory.

Lord, You will be with me as the waters I pass through,
They will not overcome me because of You.

My job is to simply trust and obey,
Then I shall rest in You every day.

"Fear not," is what You say to me,
You will be my constant victory.

You promise to always hold my right hand,
Helping me to faithfully follow Your command.

And when the circumstance seems to overwhelm me,
I shall remember You are always my constant victory.

"Praise be to the LORD, for He has heard my cry for mercy. The LORD is my strength and my shield; my heart trusts in Him, and He helps me. My heart leaps for joy, and with my song I praise Him." Psalm 28:6-7 NIV

My Cry for Mercy

Praise be to the LORD for He has heard my cry,
I cried out for His mercy that He cannot deny.

The LORD is my strength and my shield,
To Him alone my life I shall yield.

I am helped as my heart trusts in Him,
For He has freed me from the bonds of sin.

Fully He gave Himself for me,
As He hung on the Cross at Calvary.

My heart leaps for joy and has become strong,
I will give praise and thanksgiving to Him in song.

Praise the LORD! My cry for mercy He has heard,
I shall always stand on the promises in His Word!

"That Christ may dwell in your hearts
through faith..."
Ephesians 3:17

My Heart Christ's Home

To the Father of our Lord Jesus Christ I bow
my knees to pray,
That Jesus would dwell in my heart through
faith in Him today.

And that I being completely rooted and
grounded in His love,
May understand the width, the length, the
depth, and the height thereof.

And know the love of Christ which passes all
understanding in any way,
That I would be filled with all the fullness of
God each day.

Having an intimate fellowship with the Father
through His Son,
Allowing Jesus Christ to reside in my heart as
the Supreme One.

That Christ may dwell in my heart through
faith in Him,
And my heart would be Christ's home, that
place He dwells in.

"For You are my hope, O LORD God; You are my trust from my youth." Psalm 71:5

My Hope is in You LORD

My hope is in You, LORD,
You are the greatest treasure.
My hope is in You, LORD,
Your love for me is beyond measure.

My hope is in You, LORD,
All my needs You always meet.
My hope is in You, LORD,
You fill me as I sit at Your feet.

My hope is in You, LORD,
Your precious promises You freely give.
My hope is in You, LORD,
You will never fail me as long as I live.

My hope is in You, LORD,
Eternal life You have given to me.
My hope is in You, LORD,
You are my Savior and in You I am free.

"Her children rise up and call her blessed..."
Proverbs 31:28

My Mother

My Mother is a precious gift from the
Father above,
She is an example of His tender mercy and
His eternal love.

Her hands are extended to heaven every day,
She intercedes for me, and never fails to pray.

She sacrificially gives to me all I could
ever need,
She is a virtuous woman in thought and
in deed.

My mother is kind and full of God's grace,
She is loyal, dependable, and a safe place.

My mother is my heavenly Father's precious
gift to me,
She is a reflection of His love that I can
clearly see.

"Why am I discouraged? Why is my heart so sad? I will put my hope in God! I will praise Him again – my Savior and my God!"
Psalm 42:11 NLT

My Savior and My God

Why am I discouraged and why is my heart so sad?
Trouble has beset me and the suffering has been bad.

The sorrow and depression are ever so near,
The trials and the tribulations can cause me to fear.

I must trust in the Lord and depend on Him whatever I do,
Even in the dark valleys He will be with me and see me through.

And I will put my hope in the Lord God above,
I will praise Him again and give Him all my love.

Remembering He is my Savior and my God every day,
And I will look to Him as I follow Him His sovereign way.

"I thank my God, making mention of you always in my prayers." Philemon 4

No Matter Where You Are

No matter where you are,
If you are near or you are far,
I will be praying for you.

When you are up or you are down,
If you have a smile or a frown,
I will be praying for you.

Even when the road gets tough,
If it seems there is not enough,
I will be praying for you.

Then when your bottom falls out,
If then you are left in doubt,
I will be praying for you.

For the power of prayer,
Will meet your need anywhere,
I will be praying for you.

In everything you pursue,
Our God will see you through,
And I will be praying for you.

No matter where you are,
You will never be too far,
For me to be praying for you.

"And whatever things you ask in prayer, believing, you will receive." Matthew 21:22

On The Wings of a Prayer

Lord, it is coming on the wings of a prayer,
Your answer to my request, the relief of this care.

I cried out to You, Lord, my God almighty and You heard me,
I reached to heaven on my knees and touched You in eternity.

I am able to leave the boundaries of time and space,
As I kneel before Your throne of mercy and grace.

You answer according to Your will and good pleasure,
For I am to You, my dear Lord, Your special treasure.

Lord, You shall not withhold from me one good thing,
You are my sovereign Savior and my ruling reigning King.

There is nothing in all of creation too great or too difficult for You,
You spoke the universe into existence, yet You are mindful of all I do.

Thank You, Lord, for on the wings of a prayer the answer is coming,
Therefore, to Your throne of grace I will always come running.

"I will praise You for I am fearfully and won-
derfully made; marvelous are Your works, and
that my soul knows very well," Psalm 139:14

One of a Kind

Fearfully and wonderfully made by God, I am
one of a kind,
Even before the universe was formed I was
always on His mind.

Treasured and adored He knit me together
according to His will,
Orchestrating His plan for me He then prom-
ised all my needs He would fill.

Then He numbered all my days and in His book
they took their place.
He died for me that I could, at the end of my
days, behold His face.

Oh, how He loves me infinitely abundantly
beyond compare,
He gave me Jesus, my Lord and Savior, and
one day eternity with Him to share.

I am one of a kind, yes, how precious are His
thoughts for me,
If I should count them they are more than the
sands of the sea.

"…to give them beauty for ashes, the oil of joy for mourning, the garment of praise for the spirit of heaviness…" Isaiah 61:3

Our Relationship

Lord Jesus, as I look back at our relationship these past years,
I'm reminded that You have been the faithful One who has dried all my tears.

You have given me Your peace and allowed me to go on,
You have been my constant joy and my eternal song.

You have brought me through my darkest hour,
You have strengthened me by Your supernatural power.

Even as Your sheep I am prone to wonder and even stray,
You promise to never leave me and that by my side You will stay.

You have been my fortress and my high tower through every storm,
You have given me beauty for ashes and the oil of gladness when I mourn.

Always sufficient onto me is Your nev-
er-ending abundant grace,
I bow in humble submission before Your
throne, taking my rightful place.

No greater love could anyone ever have known,
That is the love for me You forever have shown.

Ever before You, Lord, I shall always worship
and adore You,
Our relationship is the one thing that will for-
ever see me through.

"In all things showing yourself to be a pattern of good works; in doctrine showing integrity, reverence, incorruptibility," Titus 2:7

Patterned After You, Lord

Lord make my life a pattern of good works patterned after You,
Placed by Your hand to do that which You have called me to do.

In doctrine showing integrity, incorruptibility, and reverence,
Then I must, upon You, Lord, place all my dependence.

I am pinned by You upon the fabric of this life,
Oh, that I would not struggle nor be filled with any strife.

That I would allow Your shears to remove that which needs to be,
And that which is left would be Your glory and Your majesty.

Fashioned by Your hand into a fitting garment of praise,
I will continue to work Your good works all of my days.

Patterned after You, Lord, to make Your will mine,
Designed into the image of Jesus by Your divine design.

"Praise be to God and Father of our Lord Jesus Christ! In His great mercy He has given us new birth into a living hope through the resurrection of Jesus Christ from the dead."
1 Peter 1:3 NIV

Praise be to God

Praise be to God the creator of heaven and earth,
Into a living hope He has given us new birth.

Our Lord, Jesus Christ, displayed His great mercy and grace,
When he died on the cross for our sins by taking our place.

Then through the resurrection of Jesus from the dead,
We are no longer defeated but share in His victory instead.

Oh the joy and the rapture that continues to unfold,
As one day soon, we shall His face behold.

Praise be to God the Father of our Lord Christ Jesus,
For the great plan of redemption that has freed us.

"…if God is for us, who can be against us?"
Romans 8:31

Precious Savior

Precious Savior, You are my all in all,
Keep me from slipping; please don't let
me fall.

I am standing on a cliff, the very edge,
You are faithful Lord to widen the ledge.

You have brought me here for a specific reason,
And I know this trial will only last for a season.

My faith needs to be proven that it is genuine,
Why and what I believe will be shaken one
more time.

As I speak these words from Your Word
let it be,
"God is for me, who, therefore, can stand
against me?"

Nothing that ever comes against me will ever
prevail,
Because Your promises are true and will
never fail.

Precious Savior, my Jesus, You are my all in all,
You won't let me slip; You won't allow me to fall.

"I have heard of You by the hearing of the ear, but now my eye sees You." Job 42:5

Quietly Sit

I cried out from the depth of this dark pit,
I heard the Lord's voice say to come and quietly sit.

From the Lord I was lovingly told,
My hand He would forever hold.

As with Job, He said He would be with me in the midst of my trouble,
He would deliver me and my portion He would miraculously double.

The Lord desires to reveal Himself to me in a personal way,
That I would truly know Him and invite Him in my heart to stay.

Now I know Him and I see Him on my side,
And all that I would ever need He will provide.

I cried out from the depth of this dark pit,
Then He raised me up before Him to quietly sit.

"I will also mediate on all Your work, and talk of Your deeds." Psalm 77:12

Reflect

Lord as I sit before Your holy throne and I reflect,
Speak to me as my wayward heart You lovingly correct.

I will meditate on the work of Your hands and speak of Your deeds,
You hold the universe together while You provide for all my needs

You are faithful to keep me and cleanse all my ways,
For You are my Father God who will keep me all my days.

In You, O, Lord, I will find a complete and satisfying rest,
I am convinced that You work all things in my life for the best.

You are conforming me into the image of Your dear Son,
And that You won't stop the work in me until You are done

Because You are working deep within my
heart it delights my soul,
For the end result is that I stand before You
righteously whole.

Lord as I sit before Your mighty throne and
reflect,
My relationship with You I purpose in my
heart to never neglect.

"Come to Me, all you who labor and are heavy laden, and I will give you rest." Matthew 11:28

Run to the Arms of Jesus

When you're feeling blue,
And you don't know what to do,
Run to the arms of Jesus.

When the enemy is attacking your mind,
And peace you are unable to find,
Run to the arms of Jesus.

When your strength is gone,
And you can't go on,
Run to the arms of Jesus.

When the bottom drops out,
And you're left in doubt,
Run to the arms of Jesus.

When you can't seem to win,
And your patience is running thin,
Run to the arms of Jesus.

When disappointment sets in,
And depression begins,
Run to the arms of Jesus.

When you're up against a wall,
And you think you're going to fall,
Run to the arms of Jesus.

No matter the problem,
Jesus will be able to solve them,
Run to the arms of Jesus.

When things are going your way,
Don't stay away,
Run to the arms of Jesus.

Whatever you're going through,
This is what you do,
Run to the arms of Jesus.

"Let us run with perseverance the race marked out for us. Let us fix our eyes on Jesus the author and perfecter of our faith."
Hebrews 12:1-2 NIV

Run with Perseverance

Let us run with perseverance the race marked out for us,
With eyes fixed on the author and perfecter of our faith, Jesus.

For we proceed by faith not by sight,
And it is only by the Holy Spirit's power and might.

We remember the battle has already been won,
Making us more than conquerors because of God's Son.

We keep moving step by step as we finish the race,
Knowing we will cross over the finish line by our Lord's grace.

Keep going dearly beloved of the Lord,
For everlasting life with Jesus is your eternal reward.

"But those who wait on the LORD shall renew their strength; they shall mount up with wings like eagles, they shall run and not be weary, they shall walk and not faint." Isaiah 40:31

Safe Harbor

You are my safe harbor; You shelter me from every storm,
Faithfully through the darkest night until the dawn of morn.

I shall wait on You, LORD; I shall run and not grow weary,
Even when the sun doesn't shine and the skies are dreary.

I can dock at Your bay of tranquility which offers me Your rest,
While I mount up with wings of eagles in order to pass this test.

You renew my strength daily by Your supernatural power,
When the hurricane comes You hide me in Your high tower.

As You direct me I shall get out of the boat, walk on water, and not faint,
Eyes on You LORD, the mighty cloud of witnesses, and the humblest saint.

You are my anchor that keeps me stable and holds me still,
I can listen to Your words of love and know Your perfect will.

You are my safe harbor, my bright guiding light,
My shelter from every storm all day and all night.

"He calms the storm, so that its waves are still." Psalm 107:29

Silver Linings

The skies are grey and there aren't any silver linings on my clouds today,
Even though the storm is raging on, I know my Lord will end it someday.

I know this darkness too will come to an end,
And the warm sunshine my Lord will send.

He faithfully calms the storm and makes the waves to be still,
He is perfecting my life and placing me in the center of His will.

His rainbow will be seen at the end of this storm,
My heart will no longer have any reason to mourn.

Blue skies will be visible when the Lord says so,
As He stretches my faith and allows it to grow.

There will be silver linings on my clouds some day,
I will wait upon my Lord, for it could happen today.

"Now therefore, if you will indeed obey My voice and keep My covenant, then you shall be a special treasure to Me above all people; for all the earth is Mine." Exodus 19:5

Special Treasure

If I will obey God's sovereign voice,
And keep His covenant as my choice,
To Him I shall be a special treasure,
To Him I will bring great pleasure.

It is so hard to imagine that this I can do,
It is a work of His Holy Spirit through and through,
A work that only He can work that allows me to obey,
And keep His covenant day by day.

That is how I can obey God's voice,
And Keep His covenant as my choice,
It is how I become His special treasure,
It is how I bring Him great pleasure.

"And when she saw Peter warming himself, she looked at him and said, 'You also were with Jesus of Nazareth.' But he denied it..." Mark 14:67-68

Stand with the Savior

Will you sit with the scoffers or stand with the Savior?
What will be your actions and your behavior?

Will you follow Jesus or warm yourself at the enemy's fire?
What will motivate you, fear of this world or holy desire?

Fear can become your master in the face of danger,
Causing you to run from Jesus and become a stranger.

For if you are a scoffer in the shadows you will deny what you know to be true,
That Jesus is the Messiah, the Lamb of God who gave His life for you.

Will you sit with the scoffers or with the Savior stand?
Will you deny Him or follow His every command?

"And being found in appearance as a man, He humbled Himself and became obedient to the point of death, even the death of the cross." Philippians 2:8

Stooped

Jesus stooped from the heights of heaven to walk as a man,
He humbled Himself in order to follow His Father's plan.

He chose to wash the disciples' feet, doing a servant's chore,
He gave every bit of Himself and then He gave much more.

You see my Lord Jesus willingly died for me,
He died a criminal's death that I might be set free.

He now sits exalted at the right hand of the Majesty on High,
For God has raised Him up to be an advocate for you and I.

Therefore, let us humble ourselves before God's mighty hand,
Stooped before our Lord and Savior living in the promise land.

"…God is love." 1 John 4:8

Such Love

Such love is beyond my comprehension,
Such love that has only a holy intention.

Such love Your life for mine,
Such love that is eternal and divine.

Such love with motives so pure,
Such love that is steadfast and sure.

Such love never contemplating His own,
Such love that never leaves me alone.

Such love with supernatural strength,
Such love that will go to any length.

Such love that never comes to an end,
Such love is my Jesus, who is my for-
ever friend.

"Therefore take up the whole armor of God, that you may be able to withstand in the evil day, and having done all, to stand." Ephesians 6:13

Take up the Whole Armor

Take up the whole armor of God and be clothed in Him,
Come before the Lord with a cleansed heart free from sin.

Stand against the wiles of the devil, your defeated foe,
Be girded in the truth of God wherever you go.

Shod your feet with the gospel of peace,
Put on the breastplate of righteousness and all struggles cease.

Wear the helmet of salvation upon your head,
Take hold of the sword of the Spirit and by the Spirit be led.

The shield of faith will quench all those fiery darts,
It will protect every one of your precious parts.

Hold fast to the mighty sword of the Lord,
That which is sharper than any two
edged sword.

Above all else pray without ceasing,
And God's peace will be your keeping.

Take up the whole armor of God and be
clothed in Him,
Withstand the attacks from without and the
attacks from within.

"So teach us to number our days, that we may gain a heart of wisdom." Psalm 90:12

Teach Us

Teach us, Lord, to remember to number our days,
That we may gain a heart of wisdom in all our ways.

Our life is but a vapor that is blown away,
Let us live today as if this is our last day.

We are as cut grass that has dried up and withers away,
Our frail bodies grow old and will fail us one day.

Our time is but for a moment, let us not walk away,
Empower us to deny ourselves each and every day.

So, teach us, Lord, to number our days,
And to follow all of Your marvelous ways.

"Oh, give thanks to the LORD, for He is good!
For His mercy endures forever.
Psalm 118:1

Thank You LORD

Thank you, LORD, for answering every prayer,
For always knowing what is best for me
because You care.

Thank You, LORD, for Your answer; the yes,
the no and the wait,
For always being right on time and never
being late.

Thank you, LORD, for causing my little faith
to grow,
For driving me to my knees and allowing my
prayers to flow.

Thank You, LORD, for Your great awe-
some plan,
For the trust I place in You even when I don't
understand.

Thank You, LORD, for always hearing my
every cry,
And for Your love for me that You will
never deny.

Thank You, LORD, for Your forever enduing
mercy and grace,
And for making heaven my final destination
and my rightful place!

"To know the love of Christ which passes knowledge…" Ephesians 3:19

That I Would Know You

Lord, that I would know You is my constant prayer,
That I would recognize that I am in Your eternal care.

Lord that I would not sink into dark despair,
That, in the midst of my circumstances, I would see You there.

Lord, that I would not grow weary and want to end it all,
That I would hear Your still small voice and answer Your call.

Lord, that I would not be fooled by the evil one,
That I would rest in the victory that was won by Your Son.

Lord, that I would grow in the most holy faith come what may,
That I would know these trials are conforming me each day.

Lord, that it is You that I would inti-
mately know,
That communion with You is the place
where I go.

"For it was fitting for Him, for whom are all things and by whom are all things in bringing many sons to glory, to make the captain of their salvation perfect through sufferings." Hebrews 2:10

The Captain of My Salvation

You, Lord, are the Captain of my salvation, the lover of my soul,
You are the one thing that I live for, that which makes me whole.

By You, my Redeemer, and for You all things exist and all things are,
All creation You created; the universe with all the planets, and every star.

You are my firm foundation, the life, the truth, and the way,
You are my awesome Savior, the Lord Almighty, my Rock and Mainstay.

You present me before God our Father in all Your honor and glory,
By your sufferings I am justified through Your great love story.

For God so loved the world that He gave His
only begotten Son,
That I could be His eternal, forever, ever-
lasting beloved one

You are the Captain of my salvation, the One
that I adore,
Your love for me is never-ending and keeps
me wanting more.

"The Elder, to the elect lady and her children, whom I love in the truth; and not I only, but also all those who have known the truth." 2 John 1

The Elect Lady

The elect lady, I am chosen by You my precious Lord,
You are the way, the truth, and the life my great reward.

I shall gird up my loins with Your truth as I walk in Your way,
I shall speak Your truth as I open my mouth each day.

I shall be a minister of Your grace, mercy and peace,
I shall not let the truth of Your word ever cease.

I shall not entertain the lies of the enemy in my mind,
Nor shall I allow his cloak of darkness to make me blind.

I shall know the truth, which will always set me free,
I shall go forth in Your truth and declare Your liberty.

I shall be governed by Your love that is without measure,
I am Your elect lady; Your priceless chosen treasure.

"And now abide faith, hope, love, these three;
but the greatest of these is love."
1 Corinthians 13:13

The Greatest of These is Love

Abiding faith in the Lord God above,
Springs forth hope nourished by His love.

Faith, hope, and love are God's gifts to me,
But the greatest is His love displayed on
Calvary.

It is this gift that I am called also to give,
Love without measure as long as I live.

Love is patient and love is always kind,
In agape love, envy you will never find.

Love does not parade itself nor is it puffed up,
For God's love is always more than enough.

Love bears all things and believes all things too,
Love hopes all things and endures all things
through.

Love never fails because its true source is from
God above,
It flows freely to us from His fountain of uncon-
ditional love.

"For to me, to live is Christ, and to die is gain."
Philippians 1:21

The Keys to Joy

The keys to joy are first Jesus, others, and then
myself as God would lead,
I know as I serve Jesus and others that the
Lord will fill my every need.

For to me, to live is Christ, and to die is gain,
That is my joy for it outweighs any of
life's pain.

Knowing he will be faithful to complete His
good work in me,
I will stand fast in the faith until He ushers me
into eternity.

Through all circumstances may I speak fear-
lessly and boldly of my Lord each day,
And in all knowledge and discernment may
His love abound in me is what I pray.

The keys to joy are Jesus first, others, then
myself, beloved one,
God will be honored as we follow in the foot-
steps of His dear Son.

"Though I walk in the midst of trouble, You will revive me; You will stretch out Your hand against the wrath of my enemies, and Your right hand will save me." Psalm 138:7

The Lifeline of Prayer

Though I walk in the midst of trouble, I shall not despair,
You will stretch forth Your hand and strengthen me by the lifeline of prayer.

You, Lord, will squash the wrath of the enemy my defeated foe,
You have established my victory through Jesus everywhere I go.

I need to stay upon my knees, humbled, and submitted to You, O Lord,
This is my position of victory praying forth Your word my holy sword.

I shall wield it to and fro to extinguish the enemy's fiery dart,
Drawing upon the lifeline of prayer, which always safeguards my heart.

You, Lord, are the power that enables me to
walk the Calvary Road,
It is Your loving-kindness that faithfully car-
ries me and my heavy load.

Your right hand will save me all of my days,
I will continue to thank You and give You all
my praise.

Though I walk in the midst of trouble upon
You I shall cast all my care,
I shall continue to pick up my conquering
weapon the lifeline of prayer.

"Behold God is my salvation, I will trust and not be afraid; for Yah, the LORD, is my strength and song; He also has become my salvation." Isaiah 12:2

The LORD is My Salvation

The valley is not so deep today therefore the darkness has to flee,
Because the LORD is my salvation, my God, my victory.

I long for the mountain top LORD, where I can find my rest,
But where I grow is in the valley where my faith is put to the test.

Help me not to be afraid LORD; give me Your strength,
For I know Your love for me has no height, depth, or length.

In my heart, precious LORD, You have placed Your song,
I will trust in You and not be afraid all the day long.

The valley it is not so deep today,
Because the LORD is my salvation and my mainstay.

"Behold, God is my salvation, I will trust and not be afraid; For Yah, the LORD, is my strength and song; He also has become my salvation." Isaiah 12:2

The LORD Is My Strength

For Yah, the LORD, is my strength and my song,
He keeps me safe by His side all the daylong.

Behold, God is my salvation I will trust and not be afraid,
No matter what the plan is against me that the enemy has made.

The LORD is my fortress, my protector, and my strong tower,
I shall praise Him, declare His deeds, and His sovereign power.

I shall worship Him, exalt Him, and sing out with a shout,
For He has done excellent things and in this there isn't any doubt.

For Yah, the LORD is my strength and my song,
Therefore by His side I know I shall always belong.

"The LORD knows the days of the upright; and their inheritance shall be forever."
Psalm 37:8

The Days of the Upright

The LORD knows the days of the upright,
He knows all about their suffering and plight.

He has counted them righteous because Jesus is their LORD,
Placing His Word in their hearts as a two edged sword.

Guiding them in His truth and knowledge His way,
Filling them with His Holy Spirit that they may not stray.

Their inheritance shall be forever without end,
And all the days their life He shall defend.

When they receive their final eternal reward,
They will give all praise and honor to Jesus, their LORD.

The LORD knows the days of the upright,
They are numbered by Him and are precious in His sight.

"If it had not been the LORD who was on our side, when men rose up against us, then they would have swallowed us alive."
Psalm 124:2-3

The LORD Who Was On Our Side

If it had not been the LORD who was on our side,
The evil men would have swallowed us alive.

Against us their wrath was kindled,
Our strength it would have dwindled.

Our soul by the waters would have been overtaken,
We would have been overwhelmed and forsaken.

But blessed be the LORD who has not given us as prey,
Who is by our side and there will always stay.

If it had not been the LORD who was on our side,
We would have been devoured; this cannot be denied.

"Therefore know that the LORD your God, He is God, the faithful God who keeps covenant and mercy for a thousand generations with those who love Him and keep His commandments;" Deuteronomy 7:9

The LORD Your God

The LORD your God, He is God, He is faithful and true,
He keeps His word, His covenant, and His promises too.

And to those who love Him, His mercy overflows,
His compassion is unceasing as His grace He bestows.

And to those who keep all of His ways,
He will keep them for all of their days.

Precious is the God of the universe our Savior and LORD,
The only living God Almighty who is our awesome reward.

The LORD He is your God faithful and forever true,
Worship Him alone as God and His faithfulness pursue.

"For with God nothing will be impossible"
Luke 1:37

The Miracle

For with God nothing will be impossible; no
not anything,
He is the creator of the universe and the mir-
acle working King.

God brought forth a miracle life to give life
eternal for us all,
This holy solitary life was predestined to save
us from the fall.

Born of a virgin in Bethlehem on that first
Christmas day.
Jesus the Son of God, the truth, the life, and
the only way.

The miracle of Jesus' birth was for us, the
people He came to save,
He willingly was crucified for our sins, buried,
and raised from the grave.

Interceding on our behalf, He is seated at our
Father's right hand,
Let us bow down, worship at His feet, and
follow His command.

Rejoice, for one holy night Jesus Christ our Savior stepped into time,
The Mighty God, the Prince of Peace, the Miraculously Divine.

For with God nothing will be impossible; His grace and mercies still abound,
We were once lost but because of His miracle at Christmas we are now found.

"The name of the LORD is a strong tower; the righteous run to it and are safe."
Proverbs 18:10

The Name of the LORD

The name of the LORD is a strong tower,
Yet, it is the sweetest most fragrant flower.

The righteous run to it and they are safe from all harm,
They shall fear not nor shall they be stricken by any alarm.

The name of the LORD is a safe and secure place,
They shall hide in it and behold God's grace.

The righteous are renewed by it day by day,
In every dimension, every direction, and every way.

The name of the LORD is our strong tower,
It is our fortress and our staying power.

"Be anxious for nothing but in everything by prayer and supplication, with thanksgiving, let you request be known to God; and the peace of God, which surpasses all understanding will guard your hearts and minds through Christ Jesus." Philippians 4:7

The Peace of God That Surpasses All Understanding

With thanksgiving to the Lord offering every-
thing up in prayer
And the peace of God that surpasses all under-
standing casts off any despair.

Wars and rumors of wars are all around,
And the peace of God that surpasses all under-
standing is easily found.

Famine and disease devouring so many lives
this day,
And the peace of God that surpasses all under-
standing is the only way.

Evil and violence seem to prevail as they fill
all the land,
And the peace of God that surpasses all under-
standing allows me to stand.

Therefore, Jesus, I patiently steadfastly continue to wait for You,
And the peace of God that surpasses all understanding keeps me in all I do.

"For I know the plans I have for you, declares the LORD, plans to prosper you and not to harm you, plans to give you hope and a future." Jeremiah 29:11 NIV

The Plans I Have For You

It is a new day My beloved, be of good cheer,
The plans I have for you are to prosper you,
have no fear.

I would never harm you; I only desire you
to grow,
That in your heart of hearts My love for you,
you would know.

My plans for you are to give you a future
and a hope,
Look to Me in every trial; I will enable you
to cope.

I will turn it around for your good; trust in
Me today,
I will be your Savior and LORD; I will be with
you all the way.

For I know the plans I have for you,
Just depend upon Me whatever you do.

"The refining pot is for silver and the furnace for gold, but the LORD tests the hearts."
Proverbs 17:3

The Refining Pot

The refining pot is for silver and the furnace for gold,
Regardless of your position the LORD'S grace you shall behold.

Dearly beloved, the LORD tests each heart,
You must put your trust in Him for that is your part.

Therefore, whatever your condition, whatever your state,
Remember to always depend upon the LORD and to wait.

The LORD will test your heart and cause your faith to grow,
With various trials that are needful this you need to know.

Their timing is perfect according to your Father's perfect will,
He shall bring about His divine purpose but you must remain still.

Many are the afflictions of the righteous walking God's Way,
Therefore, His promise of deliverance needs to be your mainstay.

The refining pot is for silver and the furnace for gold,
You are His precious workmanship, a thing of beauty to behold.

"Show me the right path, O LORD; point out the road for me to follow." Psalm 25:4 NLT

The Right Path

O LORD, show me the right path where I should go,
I trust completely in You for it is Your faithfulness that I know.

Point out the road for me to follow LORD by Your sovereign hand,
It is upon Your precious promises to me that I will take my stand.

You are the God of my salvation and upon You I wait all the day,
I will travel where You take me and seek Your roadmap as I pray.

You will always lead me on the right path this I know,
I will trust in Your unfailing love for me and I will faithfully go.

"Jesus said to him, 'I am the way, the truth, and the life. No one comes to the Father except through Me.'" John 14:6

The Road That Leads to Heaven

The road that leads to heaven is a very narrow space,
It is as wide as Jesus' outstretched arms and paved with His amazing grace.

Jesus spoke the truth when He said that to the Father, I Am the only Way.
Run to His arms of salvation and receive Him as your Savior today.

Step on that narrow road that Jesus stands upon,
And walk the path of Calvary as you journey on.

You will never regret the choice you have made to follow Him,
He will free you from all bondage and forgive you all your sin.

Jesus truly loves you for He gave His life for you,
That you might live with Him in heaven as all God's children do.

The road that leads to heaven is a very special place,
It is built upon Jesus, God's eternal never ending mercy and grace.

"To everything there is a season, a time for every purpose under heaven."
Ecclesiastes 3:1

The Seasons of Life

The seasons of life are given to us by God for a specific reason,
They are orchestrated by Him and last according to His appointed season.

In God's precious book each of our days have been written out,
His business, therefore, we must always be about.

We begin miraculously and then we rapidly grow,
His message is written on our hearts that His will we would know.

When we accept Jesus Christ as Savior we are united to Him as one,
Serving God our Father we die to our flesh and follow His Son.

Let us not become side tracked by the trials that come our way,
Rather, let us stay focused on Jesus as He transforms us each day.

We then shall be thankful because we know
God has a wonderful plan,
As He unfolds it according to His purpose as
only He can.

All these things shall cause our faith to be
refined as pure gold,
And allow our passion for Jesus to be fervent
instead of waxing cold.

We remember that our light afflictions are but
for a moment in time,
And that they are working in us an eternal
weight of glory that is sublime.

The seasons of life are given to us according
to God's good measure,
For our heavenly Father loves us and sees us
as His great treasure.

"…Behold, the Lion of the tribe of Judah, the Root of David…" Revelation 5:5

The Spotless Sacrificial Lamb

The Lion of the Tribe of Judah, the Root of David, the Spotless Sacrificial Lamb,
The Lord God Almighty, the Messiah, the Savior is who I Am.

The Righteous, Holy, Eternal One,
The Redeemer, the Living Word, God's only begotten Son.

The universe is kept by My power and held in My hand,
I created everything including every grain of sand.

I Am before the beginning and I Am without end,
I made you to fellowship with Me and to call you My friend.

Simply put your trust in Me as your Sovereign Lord,
And I shall freely give you life eternal as your heavenly reward.

I Am the Spotless Sacrificial Lamb that for
your sins was slain,
Receive Me as your Savior for I have wiped
out all of sin's stain.

"The steps of a good man are ordered by the LORD, and He delights in his way. Though he fall, he shall not be utterly cast down; for the LORD upholds him with His hand."
Psalm 37:23-24

The Steps of a Good Man

The steps of a good man are providentially ordered by the LORD,
They are filled with His blessings and abound in His reward.

The LORD delights in him and takes pleasure in his ways,
He covers him in His amazing grace all of his days.

Though he fall he shall not be utterly cast down,
He will raise him up and place upon him a glorious crown.

For the LORD upholds him with His all powerful hand,
He enables him by His righteousness to faithfully stand.

A good man's steps are ordered by the LORD
God creator of all,
Who takes delight in him and upholds him
even if he should fall.

"…weeping may endure for a night, but joy comes in the morning." Psalm 30:5

The Sunshine and the Rain

Lord, thank You for the sunshine and the rain,
Thank You for the joy and even the pain.

I know my weeping may endure for a prescribed season,
Help me to remember that You always have a good reason.

And remind me Lord that after the rain the sun is sure to follow,
And what You have for me will not be a bitter pill to swallow.

I know it all works within Your marvelous plan for me,
By faith I trust in You when what I hope for I can't see.

For joy comes in the morning of each new day,
And the future for me needs to be lived Your way.

I will depend on Your promises through the
darkest night.
And to Your everlasting arms of love I will
take my flight.

Lord, thank You for the sunshine and the rain,
Standing upon Your faithfulness I shall remain.

"In a moment, in the twinkling of an eye, at the last trumpet. For the trumpet will sound, and the dead will be raised incorruptible, and we shall be changed." 1 Corinthians 15:52

The Time Is At Hand

The flowers were red and the leaves were green,
The time was at hand, if you know what I mean.

The clouds were silver the skies were blue,
The world was making merry and hadn't a clue.

The trumpet of God will sound with a blast,
And the Lord will return for His saints at last.

Then in a moment and in a twinkling of an eye,
The dead in Christ were raised to meet the Lord in the sky.

And we which were alive and which remained,
Were translated with them and immediately changed.

Thus we shall together forever remain with Jesus our Lord,
Living in splendid tranquility and in His heavenly accord.

The flowers were red and the leaves were green,
The time is at hand, I hope you know
what I mean.

"For, lo, the winter is past, the rain is over and
gone; the flowers appear on the earth;
the time of the singing of the birds is come."
Song of Solomon 2:11-12 KJV

The Winter is Past

Once again the winter is past,
And the rain is gone at last.

And on the earth the flowers appear,
Yes, springtime is finally here.

The smell of roses fills the air,
The time of birds singing is everywhere.

Thank You, Lord, for the winters in our life,
The struggles, the trials, and even the strife.

For without them we would never know the
joy You bring,
Nor the knowledge of Your sovereign plan
through everything.

If we never suffered patiently as Your will
we pursue,
We wouldn't know how to deny ourselves,
pick up our cross, and follow You.

We would never see the sunshine after the rain,
Nor experience true joy without enduring
the pain.

For this is how we are conformed and become
like You,
It is how we can say thank You for the winter
and the springtime too.

"That Christ may dwell in your hearts..."
Ephesians 3:17

There's No Place Like Home

There's no place like home; it is our near hiding place,
Where Jesus has positioned us by His sovereign grace.

It is where we can come before the Lord each day,
And grow in the knowledge of His wisdom and His way.

Renewal and strength come to us from Jesus our Lord,
When we sit at His feet in His sweet humble accord.

Our home is the place where we can face every trial,
It is our private sanctuary as we trust Jesus all the while.

Working in God's field, we reap and we sow,
Our home is where our love is tested and allowed to grow.

Be at home with the Lord; make your heart
Christ's home,
From His providential care never allow your
heart to roam.

There's no place like home; whether near or far,
God will do His work in us no matter
where we are.

"In the beginning God created the heavens and the earth." Genesis 1:1

This Glorious Land

My eyes have seen this glorious land,
It has been created by God's mighty hand.

Freedom reigns supreme from sea to shining sea,
God bless America the "Land of Liberty."

It's a grand vision of God's providential care,
Let us continue to lift our nation up in prayer.

We faint not while we are faithfully doing good,
Thus God's plan is acted upon and totally understood.

To pursue righteousness and to love one another,
We reach out to others as a sister or a brother.

Preserving and protecting our certain inalienable rights,
We are vigilant to serve our country all our days and nights.

Dear Lord, allow my eyes to always see this glorious land,
Help me to care for His creation and follow His command.

"These things I have spoken to you, that in Me you may have peace. In the world you will have tribulation; but be of good cheer, I have overcome the world." John 16:33

This is My Doing

"This is My doing," and I, your Lord, make no mistake,
"This is My doing," and I do it for your sake.

Remember this when circumstances do not seem fair to you,
That I have your best interest in mind in every-thing I do.

"This is My doing," let My peace draw you near,
"This is My doing," I have overcome; be of good cheer.

As you are in the midst of trials and you know not where to go,
Know that I love you more than you can ever know.

"This is My doing," My beloved, never have any fear,
"This is My doing," My dear child, do I make Myself clear?

"One generation shall praise Your works to another, and shall declare Your mighty acts." Psalm 145:4

This One Generation

I am this one generation that shall praise Your works to another,
I shall declare Your gracious mighty acts above any and all other.

I shall proclaim Your greatness and Your goodness to me,
That the next generation would know the splendor of Your majesty.

I shall extol You, my righteous God and my holy King,
Thus I shall teach the next generation to worship you in everything.

I shall speak of Your grace, which is full of compassion,
And of the love Jesus Christ showed everyone through His passion.

I shall sing of Your great tender mercies for all,
I am this one generation who has chosen to answer Your call.

"For God so loved the world that He gave His only begotten Son, that whoever believes in Him should not perish but have everlasting life." John 3:16

This Picture

This picture that I paint is the word spoken from the Lord,
It is as gentle as a dove yet more powerful than a mighty sword.

My canvas is this paper the type is my paint,
The awesome scene is God's love for you His precious saint.

This picture never changes even though your circumstances do,
Remaining the same and established forever is God's love for you.

For God so loved you that He gave Jesus, His only Son,
And sacrificed His life for yours thus, your victory has been won.

Freed from sin when He died on the cross which displayed His love,
And empowered you by His Holy Spirit that He poured out from above.

His love for you has entrusted you with every
fiery trial,
That which teaches you first hand the sacrifi-
cial act of self-denial.

This picture that I have painted for you is in
God's loving word,
It is the greatest story ever told and the
sweetest message ever heard.

I am not a great artist, beloved; I simply
present this picture, a profound amazing fact,
God's love for you is His most priceless work
of art; His supreme sacrificial loving act.

"…I will refine them as silver is refined, and test them as gold is tested. They will call on My name, and I will answer them. I will say, 'This is My people,' and each one will say, 'The Lord is my God.'" Zechariah 13:9

Trails Make Us Who We Are

Trails make us who we are today,
They come as God allows, do their work, and then go away.

But not before they do the thing they are called to do,
That is to refine and perfect us as God's will we pursue.

They take us through valleys to lead us to higher ground,
All the while transforming us and making us abound.

The Lord is faithful to refine us in the fire of affliction,
And we can call on His name without any restriction.

He will answer us and say we are His own,
For we are as gold when refined and its purity is shown.

We are conformed into the image of Jesus for
all to see,
And if it takes this trial we say, "The Lord is
my God so let it be."

Yes, beloved it is true; trials make us
who we are,
And in God's book they make us His
shining star.

"Trust in the LORD with all your heart, and lean not on your own understanding; in all your ways acknowledge Him, and He shall direct your paths." Proverbs 3:5-6

Trust in the LORD with All Your Heart

Trust in the LORD with all of your heart,
Give Him every piece and every broken part.

Lean not on your understanding; His ways are beyond you,
In all your ways acknowledge Him in whatever you do.

He shall be faithful to direct your paths, every step you take,
Let His mercy and truth guide you in every move you make.

Then, beloved, write all of this on the tablet of your heart,
Trust in the LORD with all of your being, with every part.

"…for you do not stand under the law, but under grace." Romans 6:14

Under God's Grace

You are not under the law, but you are under My grace,
You have the distinct privilege of standing before Me face to face.

Grace that is given from Me freely to you,
Forgiveness of your sins and a life brand new.

Set apart by grace to have sweet fellowship with Me,
You are under My grace that has set you free.

Beloved, under My grace is the position where you stand,
Come and commune with Me; come and take My hand.

"Then we who are alive and remain shall be caught up together with them in the clouds to meet the Lord in the air. And thus we shall always be with the Lord."
1 Thessalonians 4:17

Until

Until we meet with Jesus in the clouds some day,
I will thank the Lord for you, my friend, as I pray.

Until time winds down and comes to an end,
I know I can count on you, my precious friend.

Until forever I shall forever always be,
Grateful to Jesus as together we spend eternity.

Until then Jesus gave us each other to reach out and touch,
To share our lives together for together they mean so much.

Until then we'll speak a language that others cannot understand,
Encouraging one another we'll help each other continue to stand.

Until we meet with Jesus face to face,
We can together keep running this race.

Until that sweet glorious day,
I will remember you always, my friend,
when I pray.

"Through God we shall do valiantly: for He it is that shall tread down our enemies."
Psalm 60:12 KJV

Valiantly Through God

Through our God we shall do valiantly as He empowers us to be bold,
For it is He that shall tread down our enemies, this is the truth to be told.

He faithfully fights our battles as in His salvation we stand,
And all our foes must flee at the voice of His command.

No weapon formed against us will prosper in any way,
For our God will cause us to be victorious at the end of the day.

Not by our power nor by our might but by the Spirit of our Lord,
He has totally vanquished our enemies by His two edged sword.

Through God we shall do valiantly; we shall be brave,
He shall tread down our enemies for it is His hand that does save.

"For unto us a Child is born, unto us a Son is given; and the government will be upon His shoulder. And His name will be called Wonderful, Counselor, The Mighty God, The Everlasting Father, Prince of Peace." Isaiah 9:6

We Adore You

O Lord, humbly at Your feet we stay,
We adore You each and every day.

Wonderful, beyond any measure,
You are our precious priceless treasure.

Counselor, who faithfully instructs and leads,
Upon Your sacred word the multitude feeds.

Mighty God, You are awesome in power,
Keeping Your saints hour by hour.

Everlasting Father, eternally forever,
Abba, Daddy, forsaking us never!

Prince of Peace, Jesus has overcome,
His work on the cross is completely done.

Therefore, we adore You, Jesus, Our Prince of Peace,
Because You paid the penalty for sin, guilt and shame must cease.

"…for this purpose the Son of God was manifested, that He might destroy the works of the devil." 1 John 3:8

Weakest Link

I know the devil's weakest link,
He is a defeated foe on a ship about to sink.

The enemy's downfall and complete destruction is Jesus' shed blood,
For its power has destroyed the evil one as a mighty torrential flood.

The devil with his lies can no longer frighten or deceive me,
Because my victory is at the precious Cross of Calvary.

Therefore, suited in the whole armor of God I shall stand,
With my weapons of warfare, the devil's attacks I can withstand.

And standing upon the promises of God Almighty,
I am more than a conqueror by His power and His authority.

No weapon formed against me shall prosper in any way,
I shall stand fast in the most holy faith every day.

Greater is He, who is alive and dwelling within me,
Than any fiery dart sent from the enemy.

The devil is defeated and I know his weakest link,
It is the blood of Jesus that caused his ship to sink.

"Put on the whole armor of God, that you may be able to stand against the wiles of the devil."
Ephesians 6:11

Weapons of War

You are my battle-ax and my weapons of war,
You are the hiding place that I am longing for.

You calm my heart as the battle rages on,
From the darkest lonely night through the break of dawn.

You are my sword that is sharper than any other,
Dividing the truth and laying all else asunder.

You are the helmet guarding my mind,
Therefore no greater peace could I ever find.

You are the breastplate covering my chest,
I can trust You for You will work it out for my best.

You protect me from the fiery darts with Your shield,
Allowing my faith to grow as my life to You I yield.

I can know that through You the victory is won,
And because of You all I need has been done.

You are my battle-ax and my weapons of war,
I can withstand whatever the enemy has and
even more.

"…well done, good and faithful servant; you were faithful over a few things, I will make you ruler over many things. Enter into the joy of the Lord." Matthew 25:21

Well Done Faithful Servant

"Well done faithful servant,"
You have been steadfast and fervent.

Now enter into your Lord's joy and take your rest,
You have run the race and have passed every test.

Eye has not seen nor has ear ever heard,
All that has been promised in God's Word.

The precious harvest will bring you before Him to stay,
You have lived your life for this and not turned away.

Immovable until the day your work here is finished,
Relying upon His promises that will never be diminished.

Beloved faithful servant, "Well done."
Enter in, for My blessings have just begun.

"But seek first the kingdom of God and His righteousness, and all these things shall be added to you." Matthew 6:33

What Matters Most

What matters most in my life is plain to see,
It's a loving relationship between Jesus and me.

First I must seek the righteousness of Him,
My God and my Savior who forgave me of my sin.

Then all that is needed in my life shall be added to this,
Not one good thing shall He withhold, nor one promise shall I miss.

What is needful for me is to be still before His feet,
Which will allow my relationship to grow infinitely sweet.

His peace shall be the thing that overcomes my life,
Relieving me from all anxiety and from any strife.

Yes, the thing that matters most for me shall
always be,
A loving relationship between my Savior
Jesus and me.

"And she had a sister called Mary, who also sat
at Jesus' feet and heard His word."
Luke 10:39

You Can See it on My Face

Can you tell where I have been; can you see
it on my face?
I've set at the feet of Jesus and rested in His
loving embrace.

My heart is overflowing as the tears of joy
do fall,
For He has taken every sorrow and has carried
them all.

He calms the raging winds and causes the
storms to cease,
He is the only joy that is lasting and He is my
only peace.

His peace is now my passion as I enter into
His rest,
I have chosen to walk in His will and receive
His best.

Now you know where I have been and you can
see it on my face,
I have been with Jesus, my Savior, and I am
walking in His grace.

"Hear me when I call, O God of my righteousness! You have relieved me in my distress…"
Psalm 4:1

You Heard My Call

My heart was broken and tears did fall,
You saw my distress and You heard my call.

The pain and sorrow was more than I could bear,
You healed my broken heart and removed my despair.

Those who sow in tears shall reap in joy,
For their pain and sorrow You shall destroy.

With unspeakable joy we shall overflow,
For Your love and comfort is what we shall know.

You relieved me of my distress Lord; You heard my call
My pain, my sorrow, Lord, You took them all.

"...but the just shall live by his faith."
Habakkuk 2:4

You Know it is Faith

You know it is faith when there is nothing left,
By God's power you are faithfully kept.

You know it is faith when there is no way out,
By God's power He faithfully removes
any doubt.

You know it is faith when things hoped for
you cannot see,
By God's power He faithfully causes
them to be.

You know it is faith when your ground
becomes sinking sand,
By God's power He faithfully causes you
to stand.

You know it is faith when you are forced
to depend,
By God's power He faithfully brings the trial
to an end.

You know it is faith when in every circumstance,
By God's power He faithfully causes your heart to sing and dance.

"The LORD knows the days of the upright and their inheritance shall be forever." Psalm 37:18

You Know My Days

You know me LORD; You know the number of my days,
You are my eternal everlasting inheritance and I shall give you my praise.

As I start each day from the moment I awake,
I will worship and adore You until the last breath I take.

You have done for me what no other could ever do.
Therefore, I owe my very existence to only You.

I am wonderfully and fearfully made by Your sovereign hand,
I put my complete trust in You because it is by Your power that I stand.

You know my days however many of them there shall be,
I need not fear for You are my inheritance, the One who loves me.

"Blessed be the God and Father of our Lord Jesus Christ, the Father of mercies and God of all comfort." 2 Corinthians 1:3

Your Comfort

Your comfort, Lord, keeps me from a fearful lonely night,
It allows me to cling to You and to hold on tight.

Your comfort keeps me going strong,
It gives my heart a thankful song.

Your comfort gives me peace every waking hour,
It makes me depend only upon Your supernatural power.

Your comfort keeps me secure in every trial,
It enables me to run that extra mile.

Your comfort keeps me from guilt and shame,
It equips me to rely solely upon Jesus' name.

"And we know that all things work together for good to those who love God, to those who are the called according to His purpose." Romans 8:28

Your Plan for Good

When things haven't worked out the way I thought they should,
And they haven't gone the way I hoped they would,

Then Lord, help me to remember You've placed me in this place,
That I might know firsthand the sovereign glory of Your grace.

I know that according to Your purpose all things work together for my good,
This truth is firmly established in my mind and will not be misunderstood.

That I would grow in faith, steadfast endurance, and rest in Your peace,
That none of these things would move me nor cause my joy to cease.

And in my heart I would know it is all part of
your purpose for me,
Your purpose for good, filled with hope, and
crowned with Your total victory.

Your purpose that is covered in Your love for
me that gives me Your very best,
And that You will sustain me and strengthen
me through every trial and test.

Then when things haven't gone the way I
hoped they would,
I will know according to Your purpose, You
are working it all out for my good.

"By which have been given to us exceedingly great and precious promises, that through these you may be partakers of the divine nature, having escaped the corruption that is in the world through lust." 2 Peter 1:4

Your Promises

Your promises are precious and exceedingly great,
Upon them we can depend and patiently wait.

Your promises are faithful and always true,
We can stand in the midst of trials because of You.

Your promises are enduring and steadfast,
Forever without end they shall forever last.

We lean not upon that which we think we know,
It is Your promises we hold onto as we let go.

Precious are Your promises and exceedingly great,
Fulfilled in Your time therefore upon them we shall wait.

"May Your unfailing love come to me, O LORD, Your salvation, according to Your promise;" Psalm 119:41

Your Unfailing Love

O LORD, may Your unfailing love come to me,
And the promise of Your salvation be my song of victory.

For my Jesus willingly stood in my place,
Bearing my sin and shame by His amazing grace.

O LORD, may Your Spirit fill me every day,
And my heart desire to go Your way.

For without Your power from on high,
My hopes would shrivel up and die.

O LORD, thank You for Your unfailing love that flows to me,
It is Your promise fulfilled giving me victory!

"…nevertheless not my will, but Your will be done." Luke 22:42

Your Will

O, God, that I would seek Your will,
And with Your word my heart I would readily fill.

"Not my will," is what I would pray,
"Your will be done," is what I would say.

That I would seek You, Lord, in all that I do,
Never making a decision without first asking You.

And my life would be lived in such a way,
That I would know Your will every day.

O, God, that I would seek Your will,
That I would quietly sit before You and be still.

"Yours is the day, Yours also is the night; You establish the luminaries and the sun. You have fixed all the bounds of the earth; You made summer and winter." Psalm 74:16-17 NRSV

Yours is the Day

Yours is the day, Yours also is the night,
In You, Lord, is all power and might.

You establish the luminaries and the sun,
You are our sovereign God, the Holy One.

You have fixed all the boundaries of the earth,
You are mindful of us and determined our worth.

We cannot fathom the reason why,
You hung on that cross and choose to die.

In order for us to be blameless You took our place,
That one day we could behold You face to face.

Yours is the day, Yours also is the night,
And in us dear Lord, You take delight.

"Fight the good fight of faith, lay hold on eternal life, to which you were called and have confessed the good confession in the presence of many witnesses." 1 Timothy 6:12

You've Fought the Good Fight

You've fought the good fight; you've run the race,
Now stand before the Lord and take your place.

You haven't looked back; you haven't turned away,
Receive the benefit of your reward today.

Hear these words that strengthen your heart,
Well done faithful servant; you've done your part.

Because Jesus is your Savior you can never miss,
Now enter into His heavenly and holy bliss.

Beloved, it is beyond your wildest imagination,
The joy awaiting you at your final destination.

Until then hold onto His promise that will never fail,
Free access to His throne for He has torn back the veil.

You've fought the good fight; you've run the race,
Now stand before the Lord and behold His grace.

CPSIA information can be obtained
at www.ICGtesting.com
Printed in the USA
LVHW01s0440110418
573050LV00001B/11/P

9 781498 481342